the visual guide to
CRAZY QUILTING
design

Simple Stitches, Stunning Results

Sharon Boggon

C&T PUBLISHING

Text, photography, and artwork copyright © 2017 by Sharon Boggon

Publisher: Amy Marson

Creative Director: Gailen Runge

Editors: Liz Aneloski and Donna di Natale

Technical Editor: Debbie Rodgers

Cover/Book Designer: April Mostek

Production Coordinator: Tim Manibusan

Production Editors: Jeanie German and Jennifer Warren

Illustrators: Sharon Boggon and Kirstie L. Pettersen

Photography by Sharon Boggon and Jerry Everard, unless otherwise noted

Library of Congress Cataloging-in-Publication Data

Names: Boggon, Sharon, 1956- author.

Title: The visual guide to crazy quilting design : simple stitches, stunning results / Sharon Boggon.

Description: Lafayette, CA : C&T Publishing, Inc., 2017.

Identifiers: LCCN 2016053240 | ISBN 9781617453618 (soft cover)

Subjects: LCSH: Patchwork. | Quilting. | Crazy quilts. | Stitches (Sewing)

Classification: LCC TT835 .B5138 2017 | DDC 746.46--dc23

LC record available at https://lccn.loc.gov/2016053240

Printed in the USA

10 9 8 7 6 5 4 3 2 1

Dedication

To the two people who mean everything to me: Jerry, my husband, and Eve, my daughter

Acknowledgments

I would like to thank my ever-patient husband, Jerry Everard, for his support and unfailing belief in me; my daughter, Eve Everard, for putting up with a mother who has had a fabric and thread addiction all of her life; and my dear stitching buddies Margaret Roberts (who has taught me much about embroidery over the years), Suzanne Clarke, and Dorothy Rudling for their friendship built over many happy hours stitching together as a group. I would also like to thank the Embroiderers Guild ACT for numerous tips and tricks over the years.

It is not to be underestimated how much the online community of crazy quilters has enriched my life. I would like to thank Willa Fuller and Cathy Kizerian for their tireless work in online crazy quilting groups that have proved to be a constant source of delight and inspiration. I would like to thank Allie Aller for her friendship and encouragement. My thanks also to Maureen Greeson for arranging a retreat where I met many online friends face-to-face while teaching.

And thank you to the textiles workshop at the Canberra School of Art, which taught me much about both textiles and being a professional in the field.

Contents

Part 5: Stitches and Techniques 76

::: Detail of *Diamonds Are Forever* (page 33)

Introduction

Crazy quilts originally appeared in the 1880s in England, the United States, and Australia as part of Victorian soft furnishing decor. Draped over furniture in the rooms where visitors were greeted and entertained, crazy quilts showed the skill of the person who made them. As such, these decorative quilts were for show and not meant to be used. For this reason I call crazy quilts the first art quilts.

Contemporary crazy quilting is enjoying a revival. Since there is no right or wrong way to make a crazy quilt, embracing this form of quilting can be very liberating. Crazy quilting is a wonderful way to tell a story by incorporating lace or fabric from special garments, such as a graduation or wedding dress, or adding a special hankie, antique button, or doily created by a favorite family member. You can even use silk from men's ties. You can use your computer to print photos on fabric to include with special mementos. The technique is infinitely adaptable.

Crazy quilting can be used in projects besides quilts. The technique can be used to make bags or purses, or used on garments such as vests, jackets, gloves, hats, or belts. Sewing caddies and sewing organizers make nice projects, especially if you include a needle book, perhaps with a matching scissor tidy and pincushion. Christmas decorations of all sorts lend themselves to crazy quilting: ornaments, Christmas stockings, tree skirts, wreaths, and numerous other seasonal decorations.

Personally, I love crazy quilting because apart from the wonderful array of fabrics, lace, and ribbons that I can use, I also have the opportunity to experiment with all sorts of embroidery techniques. All types of surface embroidery, beading, and ribbon work can be used, or you can draw on other textile skills such as tatting and crochet to produce highly unique projects.

The process of creating any crazy quilt project can be confusing for some. However, with this style of quilting there is no right or wrong method. It is very forgiving; you don't even have to match seams! So relax and enjoy the process.

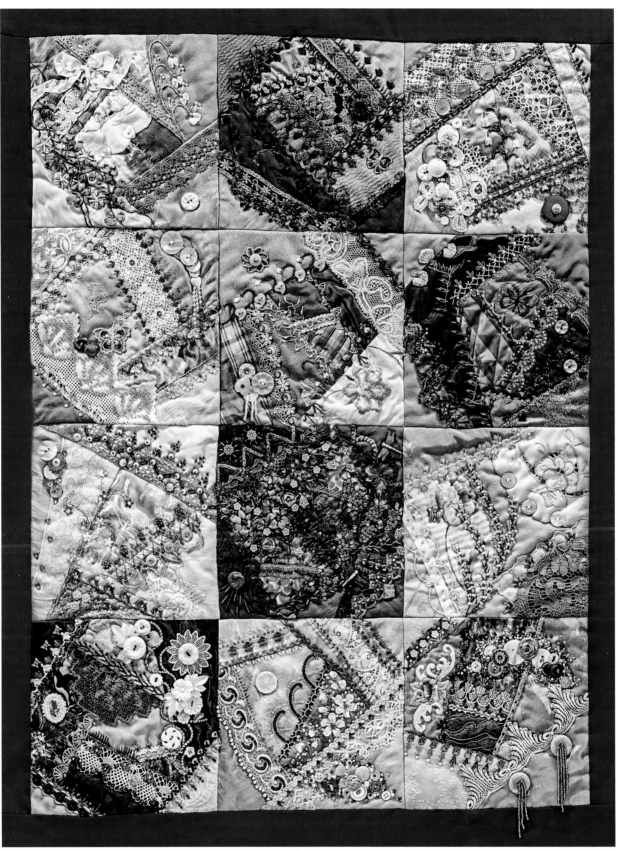

∷ *12-Square*

The Process of Making a Crazy Quilt Project

The process of creating items and blocks for a quilt can be broken down into a series of steps. Nothing is hard-and-fast in crazy quilting, as each person will have their own preferences, but these are the steps I use.

1. The first task is to piece the item or block. If it is something like a bag, I piece all sections and include lace and braids in the piecing.

2. Next I hand embroider the seams.

3. The next phase is to add embellishments such as beads, buttons, and any other doodads I want to include.

4. The last phase of the project is to assemble it.

This book follows this process, mixing the practical with theory along the way. The first section covers design and assembly, followed by how to embroider the seams. The last part covers other forms of embellishment such as beads, buttons, and charms.

Choosing a Suitable Crazy Quilt Project

For your first project, look for a simple pattern and adapt it to crazy quilting. Keep things simple until you know the process. Start on something small so you can learn the technique before launching into a larger project. When selecting a project, choose items that are easy to assemble, with flat areas that can be embellished. For instance, most bags are ideal but some can be problematic. Gussets or complex assembly can lead to beads, braids or stitching being caught in seams or tucks. Some ideal projects for beginners are cushions, bags, totes, and book covers.

However, if you choose to start on a crazy quilt block, think in terms of something between an 8″ (20.3 cm) and 18″ (45.7 cm) square. Large wholecloth quilts take quite a bit of experience to handle the many techniques.

part one
Crazy Quilting and the Encrusted Style

The Foundation Fabric

Contemporary crazy quilters often make reference to an "encrusted" crazy quilting style that takes inspiration from traditional crazy quilts but employs a combination of embroidery, beads, buttons, lace, and ribbons to produce a complex, layered visual texture. This style aims to take the viewer on a journey. By careful placement of points of interest, the viewer's eye is guided step by step.

Most contemporary crazy quilters use a foundation fabric of prewashed muslin or lightweight cotton. I have used homespun cotton, old sheets, and even the backs of old cotton shirts as a foundation. Avoid fabric that is thick, has a tight weave, or has a high thread count. Test the fabric by passing a needle threaded with embroidery thread through three layers of the fabric. If it is difficult to do this, don't use it. Find something finer, with a looser weave, because you need to be able to hand embroider comfortably through all layers.

tip Remember your seam allowance! Cut the foundation fabric to the finished block size plus a generous seam allowance. The phrase "plus seam allowance" is worth highlighting, as you would be surprised how many people forget to include it!

How Much Fabric?

You don't need yards and yards of fabric to make a crazy quilt project. You just need a variety of small pieces, such as 6″ × 6″ (15.2 cm × 15.2 cm) squares. At one stage in my crazy quilting education I was told that for an 8″ (20.3 cm) block you need a selection of 8 pieces of fabric; for a 12″ (30.5 cm) block you need a selection of 12 pieces of fabric, and so on. This is a useful rule of thumb.

I find that I like to crowd a block a little and I always add a few extra pieces. So for an 8″ (20.3 cm) block, I usually use about 10 pieces of fabric; for a 12″ (30.5 cm) block I use 14, and so on. This crowded look is not to everyone's taste. It really is up to each individual.

A crowded 8″ (20.3 cm) block of 10 fabric patches

Fabric Choice

There are no rules in crazy quilting, and theoretically you can use any fabric. My personal preference is to use thinner fabrics because I like lots of hand embroidery. You will be hand stitching through both the fabric and the foundation fabric. If the fabrics are too thick and bulky, stitching becomes a battle, which is not fun.

However, using thin fabrics may not be to everyone's taste. Your great love may turn out to be heavy bead-work. In that case you might want to choose slightly heavier fabrics so that the heavy bead embellishing will sit securely and not cause areas to sag or pull. It's a case of finding what you like and how something works for you.

If you are new to crazy quilting, I suggest that you make several small projects until you find what sort of stitching you enjoy and can relax with. Try a small block made up of thin fabrics. Then try a small project of slightly thicker fabrics and compare the experience of stitching the two.

Fabric Type

Choosing the type of fabric will be influenced by practical considerations. Will the item be washed constantly? Or is it to hang on a wall? The crazy quilt bags and smaller items I make are used, so I try to make them in such a way that they can, if needed, stand up to a very gentle washing by hand. I have also made performance costumes that had to be washed every time they were worn. These were made of cotton drill and not embellished with hand embroidery at all.

Since it is possible to make all sorts of items from crazy quilting, these are some of the considerations I keep in mind when choosing fabrics.

• If it is a garment that will be laundered often, I choose cottons and easy-care fabrics.

• Make sure that all the fabrics can be ironed.

• Too many doodads on a garment can cause problems, so use fewer embellishments but add more patterned fabrics to spice it up. If, on the other hand, the item is likely to be on a wall, you can use just about anything.

tip I prewash all fabrics, lace, ribbons, and the like that I use in crazy quilt projects. Even expensive fabric, such as silk, gets tossed in the washing machine, particularly if it has been recycled. Then if you ever need to wash your finished project you do not have to worry about shrinkage or runny dyes.

When choosing fabrics, don't forget to check vintage linens and recycled items. Include pieces from old doilies, hankies, serviettes, and ties. Use embroidered motifs on vintage linens after cutting away any damaged or stained areas and after washing the item.

Some crazy quilters only use fabrics made of natural fibers, but I use both natural and man-made fibers. There are many wonderful formal fabrics made of polyester or other synthetics. However, if you are doing a lot of silk ribbon embroidery, don't use polyester fabric. The polyester fiber will shred some types of silk ribbon. If the edges of your ribbon look worn as you stitch, the process of stitching is shredding it, and often polyester is to blame. If you plan to embellish your crazy quilting with silk ribbon embroidery, use natural fiber fabrics.

:: A crazy quilt block that features motifs from a recycled linen tray cloth

Using Men's Ties

You can recycle men's ties in your crazy quilting. They are ideal in a family history quilt as a way to remember the men in the family. Old ties are often made of silk, which makes them a dream to stitch on.

As with any recycled items, wash the ties first. I hand wash ties at least twice. After they are dry I take them apart. Many ties are hand stitched, and you can pull the stitches out in one tug if you cut the stitching thread at the top and bottom. Inside the tie you will find lining fabric. I toss the lining in the bin, but I know dedicated recyclers who use tie "guts," too! Once you have your open tie, cut out any stains, press it, and use it as you would any delicate fabric.

:: An example of crazy quilting using silk from a man's tie

Design Considerations When Choosing Fabric

Every crazy quilter finds his or her own balance of plain, patterned, and textured fabrics. To a degree, this balance becomes part of their style. For instance, on an 8″ (20.3 cm) block I may use perhaps four or five textured fabrics, one patterned fabric, and three or four plain fabrics. You do not have to follow this formula as, again, there are no rules in crazy quilting. But do think about the balance between solids, patterns, and textures when you choose your fabrics.

USING PATTERNED FABRICS

Older crazy quilts have many plain, solid-colored fabrics. However, contemporary crazy quilters have a huge range of richly patterned fabrics from which to choose. When I am piecing, I am inclined to reach for plain and textured fabrics, as these will show off stitches well. Stitching is often hidden on patterned fabrics, so I use just one or two patterned patches per block. However, if you are not keen to do a lot of hand stitching, you may wish to increase the use of patterned fabrics and cover the seams with ribbons and lace instead of hand embroidering.

When using patterned fabrics, consider the scale and type of print. I am inclined to choose prints that are roughly of the same scale. This is the safe option, but there are times when a small print looks really good against a large print.

Think about how a print may be embellished. If you are really keen on beading, think about including larger prints that lend themselves to having elements of the design picked out and highlighted in beads. Some geometric prints really sing when you add beading. For instance, if you use a print with a series of squares, you can stitch a bead on each corner.

tips If you have prints that are drowning out your stitches, these tips may help:

• Couch lengths of plain ribbon over the seam and then embroider the ribbon.

• Use a thicker thread and work your stitches on a slightly larger scale.

• Add fringe; the movement will catch the eye.

DON'T FORGET TEXTURED FABRIC!

Using textured fabric is an easy way to create more visual interest. Texture is created by the type of weave that's used during the manufacturing process, and today we have many weaving techniques to create damask weaves, brocade-type patterns, and fabrics that seem to bubble, pucker, crinkle, and fold.

Using contrasting textures introduces an element of interest from the start. The contrast does not need to be dramatic. An interesting weave against a plain fabric of the same color will make the viewer's eye pause, and that is what you want.

⠶ A block where most of the patches are textured

DEALING WITH PROBLEM FABRICS

One of the joys of crazy quilting is using wonderfully rich fabrics that are a pleasure to touch. But these fabrics can also cause the most heartache. Mixing slippery fabrics, soft silks, shiny satins, patterned silk velvets, and numerous other exotic fabrics all in one project can cause problems, particularly if pieces have been cut on the cross grain. If you are used to using quilter's cottons, these fancy fabrics may seem even more difficult to control.

If you have spent years learning how to match seams and keep a block flat and in control, exotic fabrics are likely to create frustration for you. Remember that crazy quilting is not about uniformity. You need the block to be more or less flat, but the perfection demanded in regular quilting does not apply to this style.

Many problem fabrics that slip, slide, stretch, or fray are best handled by fusing a lightweight interfacing to the wrong side before piecing the block. If a fabric is particularly difficult, interface it and use it as the first piece in a block. It will become better behaved as you add other fabrics and trap it in each seam.

Some fabrics cannot be ironed. I suggest that beginners in particular stay away from them. If you need to use a fabric that will not take ironing, use a pressing cloth to protect it when ironing the surrounding fabrics.

Sometimes a slippery fabric keeps sliding out of control. One way to tame it is to sandwich the fabric between two pieces of paper when running it through your machine. Stitch the seam and then tear the paper away. I find this the easiest method, as it does not interrupt the flow of piecing.

Sourcing Crazy Quilting Materials

Although fabric, lace, and beads are all expensive, you do not have to spend vast amounts of money to do crazy quilting. You do not need a huge amount of any one fabric. Individual pieces of fabric can be as small as 3″ (7.6 cm) square. In crazy quilting, it is variety that counts, not quantity. You do not have to repeat similar fabrics in order to unify a design.

One of the reasons I love crazy quilting is because this style appeals to my hunter-gatherer instincts. Most of my scraps are scavenged from secondhand shops, markets, old family clothing, and friends' sewing scraps. Ask local soft furnishing shops if you can buy their expired swatch books. Of course I scavenge remnant bins and specials counters, but it is via the secondhand market that I seem to find the best stuff. I pick up secondhand "after five" dresses when they are on sale. I feel crazy quilters in the past would have used anything that was attractive to their eye, so I do the same.

USING RECYCLED FABRICS AND SCAVENGED ITEMS

I recommend that fabric from a recycled garment be washed. Dirt, sweat, and the like can cause fabrics to degrade, so when I find a bargain in a charity shop, I toss it in the washing machine no matter the fiber content. That's right—silks, brocades, wedding dresses, the lot! If the fabric doesn't stand up to washing, I'm only losing a couple of dollars at the most. Once it is dry, I press it and cut out the seams, darts, and any areas of wear or staining.

In my scavenging I frequently find old hankies, men's ties, lace doilies, costume jewelry, bead necklaces, and buttons. Do not be afraid to experiment. Pull apart stuff and reuse it in interesting ways. Items can be painted, dyed, and treated to fit on a block.

I still buy commercial embellishments for crazy quilting, such as beads, nice braids, and laces. If you are new to this form of quilting, put your money into embellishments rather than fabric as it is the beads, lace, and threads that are both harder to find secondhand and to accumulate.

::: The small doily was hand dyed before incorporating it into this block.

THE DYE POT!

When sourcing materials and trims for crazy quilting, don't forget the dye pot. If you have a large amount of any one fabric, you can dye it a number of different shades or colors. For instance, pieces of a secondhand wedding dress or a prom dress can be dyed all sorts of colors and will last you a long time. You can dye lace, ribbon, shells, and buttons with relative ease at home. While you are at it, dye some embroidery threads, too. Then you will have threads that match your fabrics. Dyeing materials different colors is an ideal way to build up a crazy quilting stash. Variety is the key.

part two
Using Design to Take Your Viewer on a Journey

Some people are afraid of the "D word," but when we talk about design and composition we are simply talking about a set of ideas used to describe the relationship between various parts of an image. Often we talk about composition in paintings, but not everyone thinks in terms of composition applied to textiles. Yet when we look at a quilt, it is a visual experience, and there is no reason why we cannot apply design principles to a quilt.

Emphasis and Subordination

One of the most powerful tools you can master is to understand how points of emphasis can work for you. You hear people talk about a point of emphasis, but what exactly is a point of emphasis in crazy quilting? And once you understand what it is, how do you make one?

Emphasis can be described as an area on a block that draws attention to itself. Emphasis is the party girl whom everyone notices, or the noisy one in a group. When you look at a piece of crazy quilting, your eye immediately goes to that point, the focal point of the block. Focal points can be created by using a bright color, a piece of lace, a memento, or a technique such as an intricate bit of embroidery, a silk ribbon spray of flowers, or extravagant beading. These are just a few techniques that can create a focal point. Part of the fun of crazy quilting is that so many textile and embroidery techniques can be used to create a focal point, and it is exciting to discover a new method of using items on a project.

Usually you want more than one focal point to attract your viewer's attention. After they look at that area, you want to guide their eye to another area, and so on. One way to do this is to introduce a second and sometimes third focal point, so that the eye moves from point to point, traveling around the block. These secondary points are subordinate to the dominant focal point but are just as important. A single focal point shouldn't be so strong that your viewer's eye is locked on only that point. You want them to look around and enjoy the whole image.

So how does this work in practice? How is this theory applied to crazy quilting?

:: Make a mental note of how you view this block.
:: Think about where you look and what you look at.

:: I have circled three points of emphasis in the above photo.

1. First is the large disk of beaded tatting in the top right-hand corner. There is a lot of visual stimulation on this block, but the eye lands on the area of tatting first.

2. The second place the eye travels is to a fan-shaped piece of ribbon in the lower left corner. If this gathered ribbon was a full round of ribbon, it would be approximately the same size at the circle of beaded tatting. That would mean the two shapes would be equal in visual weight. The viewer's eye would bounce back and forth between the two and not pay attention to other things happening on the block. To avoid this, I made the ribbon fan slightly smaller in diameter and used just half a round. Cutting it in half reduced the visual weight. In other words, as a design element it is subordinate to the main point of emphasis. Also, cutting it in half meant it echoed the main shape, so it was similar but not the same.

3. The third point of emphasis is in the bottom right corner. It is actually a quarter of a round shape. The quarter-round echoes the shape of the main point of emphasis. Once again, because it is smaller, it holds less attention, so it is subordinate to the main focal point but has enough power to attract the eye to that area of the block.

I created this third point by adding bugle beads to a large flat round bead. Note that the fan of wired ribbon and the beaded tatting each have a similar large bead in the middle. This introduces the design element of repetition. The same type of bead is repeated in each case. The repetition helps to tie the three points together, yet by decorating each differently, each one works on the block in a particular way, and I also stay true to the tradition of crazy quilting, which celebrates infinite variety and innovation.

The other similarity that is repeated is the shape. The items relate to each other because they are all similar shapes. If I had used a circle, a square and a triangle, the differences would have added discord. Although each item is treated differently, they all have a central flat round bead in common. This ties them together on the block.

This visual balancing act has provided endless entertainment over the years. It is fun to see what you can do when you apply design theory to practice pieces. In the previous paragraphs I mentioned design elements such as movement, shape, repetition, and balance. In the following section I will tease these ideas out a little further.

Movement

One of the key pieces of design theory you can use to your advantage when creating a crazy quilt project is the idea of movement. Movement is the path that the viewer's eye takes when looking at something. Sometimes someone will comment, "There is a lot of movement in that piece." What they mean is that the viewer's eye is taken quickly across or around a piece. Lots of movement in a piece will feel exciting as you move your eye all around, taking in the experience quickly. A more serene piece will have less movement. The eye is guided over the piece in a steady and sedate pace. Works like this are usually subtle and are to be savored gradually. Movement is what causes these two reactions. So how does this effect crazy quilting?

I use the less strong lines within a block to direct the eye toward areas embellished with embroidery or lace or a button cluster. I aim to create a diversion from the strong diagonal lines. In the previous photo, the top area is at the intersection of two lines. These lines are felt rather than seen. The other emphasis points are placed at the end of other lines. In each case, it means the viewer's eye is given a path to follow around the block.

When working a crazy quilted piece, I usually try to slow movement down. Why? In this type of quilting there are numerous items on a block. In any one area there may be different colors and textures, small and large patches, thick and thin lace, ribbon and beads. There is plenty of visual activity going on. Some people describe this as "busy," and it is busy because there is a lot to look at! What I try to do is to control the viewer's eye and slow it down, so they have time to take in what they see.

So how do we control the movement on a crazy quilting project? The first point to understand is that every shape has its own particular energy or movement. For example, think about how a person describes a spiral staircase with their finger rising in a spiral. As their hand moves around and around, they are not describing an outline of the staircase but the characteristic line of the structure. That spiral is a description of the energy within the shape of the staircase. This line of energy is not physically real but is felt. That line is *movement*. When a person describes a staircase with their finger, what they are describing is the feeling of energy or movement contained within the shape, not the actual shape itself.

:: To see this theory applied to a crazy quilt block, take a look at
:: the underlying structure of this block.

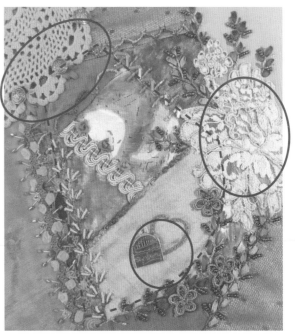

:: The largest is the area of light green lace. The viewer will then
:: notice the yellow doily in the corner. I placed it in the corner
:: so the viewer will notice it, but then their eye is deflected
:: downward, back into the block, to continue on their journey.

In quilting, we talk about flat shapes. The eye feels at ease running around the edge of the shape. The boundary of the shape has a certain energy about it. This energy creates movement around the edge of the shape.

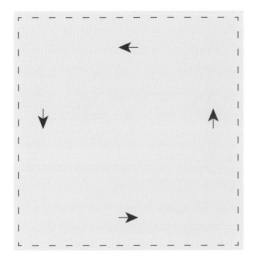

Each shape has it own energy and movement. A circle has an energy that loops around and around.

Our eye will follow the edge of a triangle, too. Irregular shapes are the same; we appear to follow the boundary of the shape in order to take in information and make sense of it.

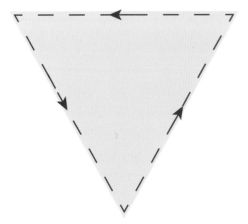

In crazy quilting, you want the eye to break away from each individual shape and move on. But how do you make that happen? If you place another object outside the shape, your eye will leave the boundary of the shape.

How does this apply to crazy quilting? If every patch is embroidered around the edge, as in traditional crazy patchwork, the eye travels around each piece. However, in contemporary crazy quilting, we introduce lots of other elements in the form of lace, ribbons, beads, buttons, and so on. If there is something that catches the viewer's attention outside of the shape, then the viewer's eye will behave differently, giving him or her a different experience. The eye runs along the side of the shape, then jumps the boundary, continues to the space outside the shape, and looks at the object that attracted it. This type of path can be used to direct the eye to a different area of a block and affect the movement of a piece.

Movement is achieved by directing the eye along a path. We guide the eye by carefully placing items of interest just outside a patch. In doing so, these elements become aspects of the design. The viewer's eye is deflected from following the edge of the patch and continues to areas of the block that you, as the creator, want them to look at.

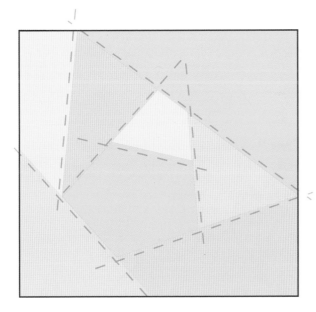

An unembellished crazy quilt block consists of patches, each shape with its own boundary. It does not have a compositional path. This can be a bit disconcerting for a beginner. I have seen students who are used to regular quilting get very frustrated at this stage, because a freshly made, naked crazy quilt block looks nothing like the finished, dressed item. In crazy quilting, the pieced block is just the first layer in the process.

A second reason for frustration is that the eye drifts over the block without settling in any one area, because the shapes are fractured, asymmetrical, and irregular. When you look at the block, your eye runs along the dominant lines created by the patches. There are always exceptions to this, but generally the eye does not really know what to land on, so it scans the block trying to decide.

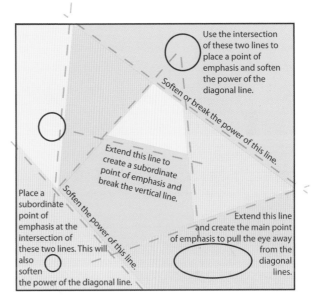

The aim is to use these directional lines to reinforce the main points of emphasis. On this block there are two strong diagonals created by the bottom left corner patch and top right corner patch. They both produce a diagonal line that takes the eye right off the block. What is needed is a technique to break or weaken the visual power of these lines. We need to make the eye of the viewer swerve off of them in order to look at the rest of the block.

tip If you are trying to knock back a dominant line on a block, look at the lines created by the other patches and ask yourself, what do they do and where do they go? Can I make any of these lines work for me?

Using Repetition to Create Balance

A composition can be made stronger by using repetition. Repeating and echoing elements on a block is a way of pulling the block together, as, at some subconscious level, the viewer picks up these echoes. They help to blend individual elements into something that is visually pleasing.

A crazy quilt block is made up of a number of shapes—the fabric patches. Some of the patches will dominate over others. The difference between shapes might be size; one patch might be larger than the others. Or it could be texture, as the eye might be drawn to a particularly shiny area, a velvet patch, or an area of lace. A strong color might attract the eye, or the fabric could be lighter or darker than the rest of the block. One particular patch might be patterned. You might say one patch just jumps out at you. In other words, the block is out of balance. There is nothing wrong with that; this creates variety and energy. But you do need to see it and understand how you might counter that patch a little and pull it into line—in other words, how you might balance the block.

One way is to repeat a color or motif that is already used on another part of the block. For instance, if you have a red patch, add a little of that red to another part of the block. It does not have to be red fabric in the construction of the block. You can add it later in the process. For example, you could embroider a red seam on the other side of the block or add a red button. It is a handy thing to remember, as it often takes just a little of the same color to pull a block together.

See if you can count how many times I used curved lines in this block. I used curved pieces in the doily and the lace in the bottom right corner. I also chose a pink braid made up of a series of curves. The straight-edge braid is patterned with a series of curved lines, and I emphasized the pattern by embroidering curved lines along its edge. The spray of organic-like growth is also curved and of course the mother of pearl buttons are repeated along a curve. My point is that one design element, in this case a curve, can be repeated in various forms to create a block that is harmonious. Echoing and repetition are both very powerful design tools, particularly for crazy quilters. I will draw attention to aspects of balance throughout the book, but as you read, note how many times it is used.

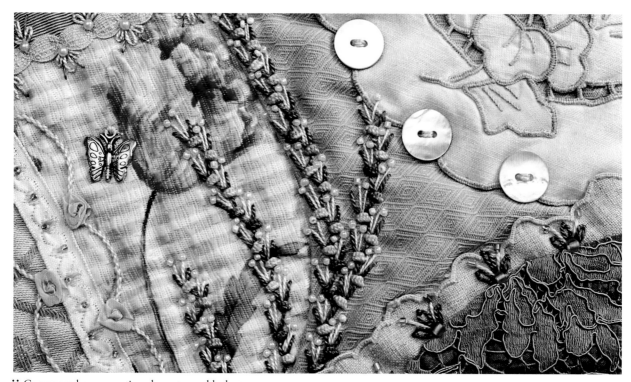

:: Curves used as a repeating element on a block

Using Color

Crazy quilters can choose to create a project using just a few colors or dive in and have a glorious multicolored rainbow. Pastels, bright jewel tones, or swatches taken from the latest fashion or interior decorating magazines can dominate a color scheme. You can take your color inspiration from a season of the year, such as the colors of spring or the chill of winter. Blocks can be bright and contemporary or the rich, dark colors of the Victorian era. You can have extremes of tonal value to add drama and energy or subtle shifts in tone that soften and sit together in a quieter, more relaxed manner. The possibilities are endless.

With so many choices, some people feel lost and unable to make a decision. There are a few tricks to make choosing colors easier. I will introduce you to a couple of ways of working with color. A little color theory will help you understand why some combinations of color work and why other combinations don't. It will also help you think through why a block is not working and then give you some strategies for fixing it.

COLOR CHOICES

How to go about choosing colors for anything is a huge subject. Books have been written about the topic and careers have been built on handling color well. Some people have studied color all their professional lives and declare, with the same passion of a young student, that they are still learning about color. Ultimately, color choice is up to each individual. Color will set a distinctive stamp on your work and will add personality to your stitching, because the colors you choose are the ones you like. They are what make your heart sing.

For some, the idea of color theory sends them running. They enjoy the tactile experience of handling fabric, and they go directly to setting one color against another until they come up with a combination that suits them. There is nothing wrong with working that way, but there may be times when you feel a little stale or think it might be fun to do it in another way.

COLOR SCHEME INSPIRATION FROM LIFE

A good, quick way of finding a color scheme is to select a favorite patterned fabric. The trick is to find fabrics that match the colors in the fabric. Once you have about five colors, you will have your color scheme for a block.

When selecting colors, also pick out lace, braids, buttons, and threads that will match the colors. It is frustrating to piece a project only to discover you don't have the right colors to embellish it. Another advantage to picking embellishments at the same time is that you can insert them as you piece your block. Thus the ends of each piece of lace or braid can be neatly tucked into the seam allowance.

The subtle paisley fabric in a man's tie inspired this color scheme. I chose colors found in the pattern.

Often while looking for fabrics that match a favorite photograph, you will find similar fabrics that almost match. They may not go with the print exactly, but they will often make a second block that will sit comfortably next to your first. One block inspires a second, and then a third, and so on. Choosing fabrics is a lot of fun and can give you hours of relaxing pleasure.

You can find inspiring colors in just about anything you see. I look at things like crockery, books, magazines, or decorative items for the home. Photographs can be a wonderful source of inspiration. Find a photo with interesting colors. Don't get seduced by the subject of the photo—just look at the colors.

:: This photo inspired the autumnal toned block.

:: An autumnal toned block inspired by the photograph

Match some of the colors in the photograph with a selection of fabrics. Pick out six to ten colors. Don't worry about trying to match every color in the photograph. Choose two or three dark colors, two or three light colors, and two to four midtones. Pull out your scraps of fabric

and match them against the image, looking carefully at what happens when you place these fabrics side by side. Also include lace, ribbons, and items you may want to add to the block. In handling the materials and placing one next to another, your color scheme will evolve.

USING A COLOR WHEEL

Some quilters do not think they respond to color via color theory. They get annoyed that they cannot match a fabric color exactly to a color wheel. Always work from your experience and with the materials you have at hand. The idea is to apply the theory to your fabric, not your fabric to the theory!

Most fabrics are not a pure color, such as a pure red or blue or yellow. They are also not a pure hue. *Hue* is a term used for color. So when people ask what color something is, they are asking what hue it is. Instead of being a pure hue, such as the colors we see on a color wheel, fabrics are often different tints, tones, or shades of a color or hue. This affects what we do with them.

VALUE: TINTS, TONES, AND SHADES

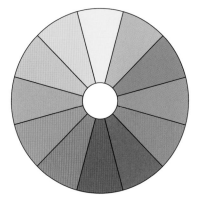

The light end of the scale has white added and is called a *tint*.

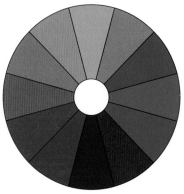

If you mix gray to the colors, you get *tones*. Tones sound dull but actually create very complex and subtle color combinations. Most fabrics are tones rather than pure colors or hues.

The dark end of the scale has more black added and is called a *shade*.

⋮⋮ For a dramatic block, use values that are far apart—in other words, extreme tints and shades. This block has light fabrics against dark fabrics, making it very dramatic.

⋮⋮ For a subtle block, choose colors that are closer in value, and incorporate many color tones.

Value is what we see as the lightness or darkness of a color. When applied to quilting, we often speak of the relationship between the light and dark patches of fabric. This is speaking of value.

tip Squint your eyes when looking at the fabrics. The patterns and textures will blur, but you will be able to see the value or tints and tones.

USE A DASH OF COLOR THEORY

Color theory creates a practical, logical way of thinking about color and a framework to start from. It allows creative choices to be made in a structured and thoughtful manner. A color wheel is a handy tool that enables people to explore the relationships between colors. Bring out your fabrics, laces, ribbons, and goodies, and match their colors against each other and the color wheel.

Everyone has encountered a basic color wheel in school and has been taught that with the three primary colors we can mix all other colors. Colors mixed from the primaries are called *secondary colors*. Mixing one primary and one secondary color that are next to each other on the color wheel forms *tertiary colors*.

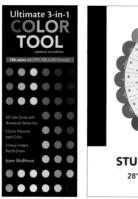 

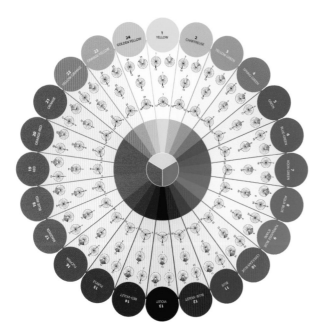

MONOCHROMATIC COLOR SCHEME

Some of the most beautiful crazy quilts I have ever seen have been monochromatic. A *monochromatic color scheme* uses different tonal values of a single color. By tonal values I mean that there are pieces in the block that are darker and lighter, but they are of the same color. Many quilts that feature family lace collections or celebrate a wedding are of neutral tones and often monochromatic.

Some stitchers start crazy quilting with a monochromatic color scheme because they feel they can learn all the other techniques associated with crazy quilting first and deal with color later in another project. To some degree this is a false security, because to make a monochromatic crazy quilt block work, you still need to vary tints, tones, and shades (refer to Using a Color Wheel, page 24) as well as texture to create a visually interesting block.

When planning your block and choosing your threads, ribbons, lace, and buttons, make sure you think about the tonal values of those items, too. Many quilters naturally reach for a range of light and dark fabrics but forget to do the same thing for lace, ribbon, and braids. Also consider the texture of the fabrics as you make these design decisions. Setting up contrasting textures, such as shiny against dull or a woven brocade against a quilter's cotton, can be as interesting to see as contrast in tonal value.

If you want to make your block sing, think about textural contrasts. You may have fabrics that are the same color, but one has an interesting weave and another is smooth. If you set these side by side on a block, you create an interesting contrast of texture. Or you may use quilter's cotton with satin or a small subtle print against a plain fabric. In each case, the color is the same and the visual interest is created by the contrast in texture. The contrast is subtle but gives the block life.

∷ A monochromatic block with a contrast of texture

∷ A monochromatic block with a tinge of color

The middle patch in the top left block is made up of a piece of textured fabric next to a piece of quilter's cotton. The interest is created by the contrast in texture. I added a braid to cover the seam that was thick and obvious. I then added some antique lace over the piece of fabric above this area. The lace is light and delicate in stark contrast to the braid. In the lower left corner there is a different vintage lace that has a small, fine pattern. In the top right I used some lace that has a much larger pattern. Once again, this is a contrast in texture rather than a contrast in color or shade. Throughout the block, the main contrasts are of texture. Even the beads and buttons add another type of textural interest.

There is nothing wrong with introducing a smidge of color. There is no rule that says you must stick to a totally monochromatic color scheme. In my own stitching, I often use a little tinge of color to create subtle contrast. In the case of this next block, you can see how, once again, I used braid and lace against textured fabrics.

COMPLEMENTARY COLOR SCHEME

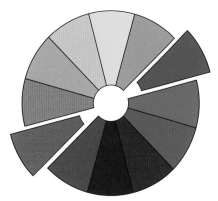

Red and green are complementary colors.

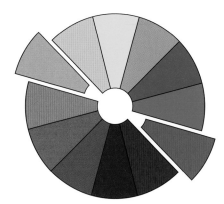

Blue and orange are complementary colors.

Complementary colors sit directly opposite each other on the color wheel. When you use a complementary color scheme, you create a strong dramatic contrast.

When applying complementary colors to a crazy quilt block, I usually use tints and shades of the complementary colors. From a color theorist's viewpoint, fabric colors are rarely pure colors, and we usually use fabrics from our stash that are tints, tones, and shades.

The techniques used in crazy quilting mean the end product is a highly decorated, visually complex item. Strong pure colors, when heavily decorated and used in combination with lots of beads, can produce a very dynamic quilt that is loaded with energy and pizzazz but is more difficult to harmonize.

················· NOTE ·················

Apply these color theories with fabric in hand, and adapt and change them accordingly.

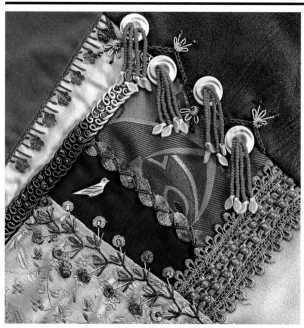

The blue is almost the color seen on a color wheel and the light blue is a good clear tint. The oranges, on the other hand, are a bit rusty and dark. The closer the colors are to pure hues, the more dramatic a block will be.

This block is also the same complementary color scheme but with more shades. The overall block is slightly darker. Darker blocks do not need to be dull, as this one demonstrates. Because it is a complementary color scheme, it is still dynamic and interesting.

SPLIT COMPLEMENTARY COLOR SCHEME

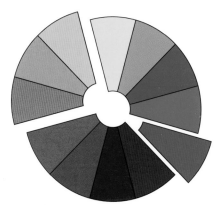

Split complementary colors

A *split complementary color scheme* uses the three to five colors adjacent to the base color. Some people find a split complementary scheme easier to handle. It has the same strong visual contrast yet is not as domineering as a true complementary scheme.

When I went to my stash, I found if I moved my three split colors around the wheel a bit I liked the result better. These theories are great to use as jumping-off places, and if they inspire you, they have served their purpose.

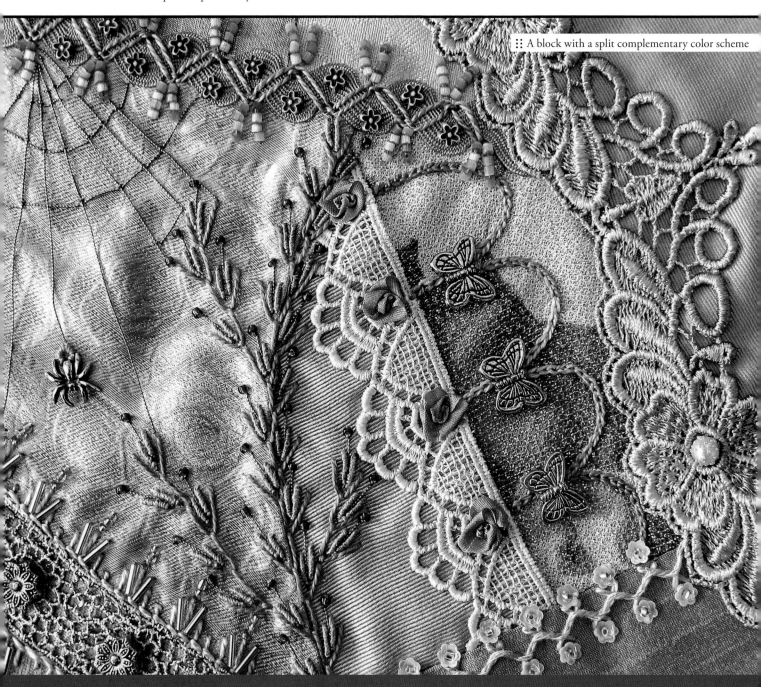

A block with a split complementary color scheme

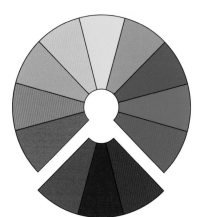

Analogous colors

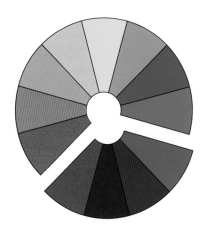

The other way to increase interest is to add more colors. You still have all the advantages of an analogous color scheme but have a little more to play with.

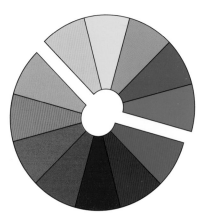

This is the color wheel for the analogous blocks below, so that you can see it applied to crazy quilting.

Analogous colors are any three or more colors that are side-by-side on a twelve-color wheel. If you are new to using a color wheel, this type of color scheme is good way of starting because they usually harmonize well together.

As a color scheme, they are comfortable but can be a little predictable. To counter this, choose one color as a dominant color and use a little more of it.

This color scheme is bright and feels like summer. When I went to my fabrics, I had two options. This first is light and airy because there are many *tints* in the block.

This darker block is constructed of *shades* found in the color scheme. I have adapted theory and used shades of green and gold.

EMBELLISHMENTS

As you piece a block, don't forget to select lace, thread, beads, and buttons to harmonize with the colors in the fabric patches. Think about color not only as you piece your project but also during the hand embroidery and embellishing phases.

tip **Storing Threads, Lace, and Beads in Color Groups**

Many people keep their threads sorted by type; for instance, all stranded cottons together, all silks together, and so on. I sort everything by color. When I am looking for a particular color, I go to that box. I also do the same for laces and beads. I store lace in plastic zip-top bags and beads in clear plastic containers, all sorted by color.

⁝ Select lace, braids, and buttons that match your color scheme.

Using Composition and Design to Manage the Bling!

The goal of this book is to provide design skills for all quilters interested in crazy quilting. Have you ever looked at a crazy quilt and felt like it was jumping out at you? Did it make you want to step back, or did you feel that it was "too much"? All those rich fabrics have noisy personalities. Those beads are a shimmery seductive lot of party girls. And the buttons—oh, buttons like to be the center of attention! Combined, this crowd makes so much noise you can't make sense of what is happening.

The secret to controlling this crowd is to manage the underlying visual structure. It is one thing to declare loud and proud that there are no rules in crazy quilting and another not to have an underlying structure. By this I mean a visual structure—something that will allow a viewer's eye to move from one area to the next. Metaphorically it would be nice to be able to take the viewer by the hand and say look at this, and then this, and so on around the block. In other words, guide their eye from one point to the next to make the experience of looking at your work pleasurable.

In crazy quilting, there are many elements to a block. As a quilter you are dealing with fabric of different colors, textures, and patterns, but you are also using embroidery in different colors and textures. Then on top of that, materials such as lace, ribbon, braid, buttons, charms, and beads are added. This cacophony of materials is visually energetic, to say the least.

When a quilter uses design principles to create an underlying composition in a block, the viewer will first look at a point of emphasis, then follow a path from one point to the next. In this case, your piece will be perceived as balanced, unified, and, more importantly, enjoyable to look at.

Composition is a set of techniques that makes the various materials on your block work together and read as a coherent whole. Using the formal elements of design, such as emphasis, movement, balance, and repetition, will help to unify and "pull a block together" visually.

The block can still be heavily embroidered and beaded, but the embellishment is integrated and composed to work for you instead of against you.

Many quilters apply design principles intuitively, particularly when selecting color and fabric. They feel confident and enthusiastic as they put color against color. However, when they move to the next stage of the process, that of embroidering the block, some are stalled. Something might not look quite right, they feel ill at ease with the block, and they put it down; the project stalls. In this situation, a little knowledge of design and composition can help.

A little design theory can aid you in making creative decisions. Because you can look at each element, it makes you focus on one decision at a time. In other words, it narrows the number of creative decisions you have to make at that point in time.

Composition and design theory are a set of tools that you can use to design a project from the start or apply when you get stalled. That said, it is useful to remember that theory is a tool used during the process and is not the sole reason for the project. You don't bang a hammer on a bit of wood just for the sake of it. You use a hammer when you need to hammer in a nail. Otherwise, the hammer stays in the toolbox. Although I advocate using theory, I don't allow theory to dictate totally what I do. In any creative practice, it is important to follow creative intuition, too. Theory is something to use when you need it, not something that dominates.

The importance of creative intuition should never be underestimated or dismissed. Gut reaction is probably the right way to progress 90% of the time. Creative intuition is unique to each individual. With experience in crazy quilting, that intuition will provide a unique spark, an individual style. My point is to encourage people to have confidence in their intuition and in due course discover a personal style. But in the meantime, if they get tangled up in knots, a little theory can help.

::: *Diamonds Are Forever*

part three
Piecing a Crazy Quilt Project

There are many methods to assembling a crazy quilt block; use just one or combine various methods. There are actually no rules in crazy quilting, which means there is no right and wrong way of piecing a block.

Stitch-and-Flip Foundation Piecing

Most contemporary crazy quilters stitch fabric patches to a foundation cloth using a method called *stitch-and-flip foundation piecing*. It is a very simple method that has a number of advantages.

- It is quick.

- It is a free-form type of piecing, so there is no marking or using templates.

- Because you are using a fabric foundation instead of paper, you do not have paper to tear away.

- The seams do not distort. Often in the process of making blocks, you will use fabrics that are cut on the bias; this can cause distortion along a seamline. With fabric foundation piecing, you don't have this problem.

- The foundation fabric adds strength, so beading and embellishing is not a problem.

This method produces a different block every time you do it. In fact, it is difficult to reproduce exactly what you have done before.

FOUNDATION FABRIC

Your foundation cloth should be a lightweight cotton muslin, or if you recycle, you can use fabric from worn bedsheets and pillowcases. Most of my quilts have a foundation of old recycled fabrics. Cotton is preferable, because you need to be able to iron it. Steer clear of using shiny, slippery synthetic fabric, because the purpose of a foundation cloth is to provide a stable base.

When choosing a foundation fabric, make sure it is thin, but not so thin that it will tear easily. You will be hand embroidering through the top patch of fabric and the foundation cloth. If the combination of fabrics is too thick, you will tire or get frustrated at pulling your embroidery thread through. Apart from the fact that it is hard to create pleasing embroidery on thick, bulky seams, if the hand embroidery is no fun you will soon become frustrated and tire of the project.

NOTES

Choose a block size you are comfortable with. I find any block between 6″ (15.2 cm) and 12″ (30.5 cm) is comfortable and does not take too long to complete.

Make sure your fabric has been washed and will not shrink.

Cut your foundation fabric square on grain (not bias) and add a seam allowance of at least ½″ (1.3 cm) all around the block. For example, for an 8″ (20.3 cm) square block you will need a 9″ × 9″ (22.9 cm × 22.9 cm) piece of fabric.

tip Why such a large seam allowance? Your block may start off flat and square, but when you hand embroider it and add beads and so on, it can pucker slightly and in some cases pull slightly out of shape. If you have a large seam allowance, you will be able to trim the block square before assembling the quilt. Leave yourself some wiggle room.

PIECING METHOD

There is no hard-and-fast rule about this, but the stitch-and-flip method works best if you start with a fabric patch that has an uneven number of sides. A piece with five or seven sides is ideal. If you are a beginner, work with five sides until the process feels natural to you.

tips

- Generally I try and use similar-weight fabrics on a project, as this saves headaches when it comes to assembling. I try to avoid the situation where I have to piece together a thick block to a thin block. For instance, when a block with thick velvet down one side needs to be stitched to a block with thin, shiny satin, it can lead to frustration. To avoid this, I keep the weight and thickness of all the fabrics about the same.

- Sometimes, however, there is a fantastic bit of velvet or tapestry I simply want to use. It sings to me! In this situation, I start the block with the special but problematic fabric. The other pieces will be added around it, preventing it from ending up on an outer seam.

- Use a good quality machine thread. I don't spend time obsessively matching thread to the color of each patch added to the block. Instead I think about tone. For light fabrics, I use white or cream thread; on darker fabrics, I use black or gray thread.

- It doesn't matter if you work in a clockwise or counterclockwise direction, as long as you don't change direction during the piecing.

1. Cut a small piece of fabric to an uneven shape of 5 or 7 sides.

2. Place your fabric on your foundation fabric slightly off-center, right side up. If you place the patch a little off-center, the block will be irregular from the start. This asymmetrical approach lends itself to creating dynamic areas, so don't fear being a little off-center.

3. Start with the longest side of the first patch. Cut the second piece of fabric so that it has one side at least as long as the longest side of the first patch.

4. Place the second piece of fabric facedown over the first patch, lining up one edge. The fabric pieces do not need to have the same size or shape, just 1 common edge. You can trim later or trim as you go.

5. Set your machine's stitch length to an average stitch size and sew along this 1 edge. Make your seam about ¼″ (0.6 cm). Sew through both fabric layers and the foundation fabric.

6. Trim the seam allowance. When hand embroidering a block, you are embroidering the fabric, the seam underneath, and the foundation fabric, so try to keep the seams trimmed and as lightweight as possible.

7. Flip the top fabric open and press.

8. Cut a third piece of fabric with one edge long enough to cover a side of the first 2 pieces.

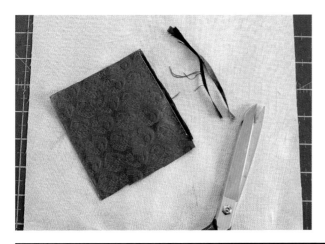

9. Lay it facedown and sew.

10. Trim, flip, and press. See why it's called stitch-and-flip? At this stage, you may need to even an edge before adding the next patch.

11. Add the next piece of fabric.

12. Continue adding patches. As you work, press each piece and trim all seam allowances. Try to vary the width of each patch of fabric, as this will add variety and interest to a block. Larger patches mean you will have room for embroidery and embellishments.

13. As you get to the edge of your block, trim away the excess fabric so you can see the balance of the block as you work.

14. Keep pressing each seam and trimming as you go.

15. It is common to end up with small corners. Just add more fabric to cover them.

16. After you cover the foundation fabric, stitch around the edge of the block. This stay stitching will help prevent the block from stretching.

tip I stitch around the block at the seam allowance line. It reminds me not to embroider or embellish outside that line. Otherwise, I am likely to break my machine needles on beads when I assemble the quilt!

Some people see a long strip of fabric in a crazy quilt block as a compositional problem. A strong directional line across a block can mean the viewer's eye will just shoot off the block. If, as you piece, you discover that you have inadvertently created a block with a particularly long strip of fabric, here are a couple solutions.

Option 1

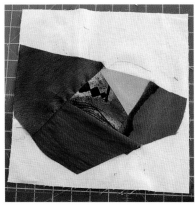

Join multiple pieces of fabric together. Make sure the scraps have a common edge.

Stitch this section of patched fabrics to the block as you would any other piece of fabric, and press open.

Option 2

Another solution is to fool the eye and draw the viewer's attention toward another visual element, such as a lace motif, a piece of interesting embroidery, a cluster of buttons, or a trail of beads placed on or near the line.

These solutions both break the energy of the dominating lines.

Embellishment Decisions

There are many wonderful things you can include on crazy quilt blocks, and for anyone who is new to the style, it can be a little overwhelming. If you feel that the options are just too many, pull back and choose one or two things to experiment with. For instance, try a project with just lace and braids. As you gain experience, you may want to add more; before you know it, you'll be using all sorts of embellishments and wondering why they felt so daunting.

Some quilters like a particular ratio of lace to fabric and choose to cover only a percentage of the seams with braids or lace. So, for instance, if you have ten seams to cover on a block, choose two and cover them with braid or lace. Once you have developed a sense of pleasure using these elements, you can increase them, if you want.

Including Lace, Ribbon, Braids, Doilies, Hankies, and More

There are many items you can add to a crazy quilt block. Not only is it fun, it makes for interesting crazy quilting. Some common items are lace, ribbons, braids, doilies, the corners of hankies, and prairie points. Other items might be photographs printed on fabric, scraps and samples of embroidery, bits of cross-stitch (a great way of using old projects), or sections of embroidery found on old tablecloths or tray cloths. Once you start crazy quilting, you'll spend your days noticing all sorts of things that can be included in your next project.

I will share examples of crazy quilting that include items such as lace, braids, ribbons, hankies, and doilies to give you ideas about not only what to include as you piece but also how you might treat them once you have them on a block.

I add these extras as I assemble the block. I like the edges of doilies and hankies—and the ends of lace, ribbon, rickrack, and braids—to be hidden in the seams, so I add them as I piece. As you assemble your block, use a few pins to keep them in place during the sew-and-flip process. Sew them into the seam; then trim.

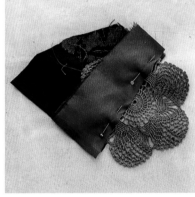

⠿ Add extras into the sew-and-flip seam.

I have found that with doilies, hankies, and the like it is really very easy to misjudge how much you will need. It is real tragedy if you make a mistake when cutting something like a hankie that is a memento of a family member, so I stitch the item into the seam first, then trim.

For larger elements, I tack or baste them into place so they don't flap about as I assemble the block. It is really easy to catch them under the sewing machine foot and stitch them where you don't want them stitched.

tip When using braids or any thick items, keep them to the middle of the block. Thicker items can be bulky at the edge of a block and cause bumpy, unattractive lumps along the seams when you assemble your project. So keep bulky braids away from the outer edges of a block. This is particularly true at the corners of a block; lumpy seams and neat corners do not go together.

USING LACE YARDAGE

As you piece your block, think about how you can use lace on your seams. What's wonderful about using lace is that you do not have to be a fantastic embroiderer to embellish it, and you can use lace to quickly cover a seam. Don't be afraid to use large pieces of lace, either. You can use quite large pieces on a block before the block looks out of balance. As you piece, also think about how you might embellish the block. You do not have to make any hard-and-fast design decisions at this point, but just be aware of some possible methods of embellishment and how that might effect the composition of a block.

Lace yardage is mainly a linear element on a block, which means it will guide the viewer's eye along the seam. These paths can be wide or thin, zigzagging or wandering. Often these paths echo the main lines found in the patterns of the lace, ribbon, and trim. This means that careful placement can help you compose your block.

Let's look at what can happen on a block when you use lace. The amount of zigzagging and wandering a viewer's eye will do varies, but the viewer will generally follow the path as demonstrated by the dashed line.

This block hosts a lace collar balanced by embroidery and beads worked on the other side of the block.

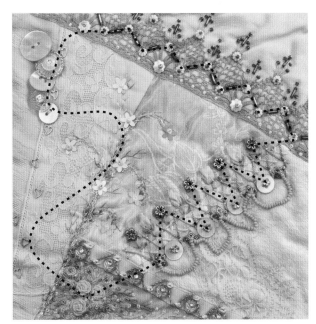

The eye zigzags along the lilac ribbon, traveling towards the top right corner before turning to travel along the blue lace. At the top left corner the eye is attracted by the buttons, then travels down the antique collar back to the base.

The amount of movement the viewer's eye makes will differ with each person, but note how the embroidery, beads, and buttons all encourage this movement. When you follow the pattern of lace with beading or stitches, or echo the line, the repetition will strengthen the line, directing the viewer's eye to a place on the block that you want them to see. For comparison, look at the lace collar on the left side of the block. It is a large piece, covering nearly a third of the block, but it does not dominate because other things on the block catch the eye. I treated the collar more delicately, because it is a beautiful fine piece and I wanted to let it speak for itself. Take a look also at the wide unembellished lace in the bottom right corner. It is quite wide, yet it does not dominate. You do not have to cover everything in beads and stitches.

ECHO PATTERNS FOUND IN YOUR LACE

When you choose your lace, think about how you might echo and repeat the pattern found in the lace.

This blue lace was embellished with beads and fargo roses. It was extended with embroidery and more beading that echoes the pattern established by the lace. This repetition of pattern makes the line stronger.

Here, the lace sits against a busy patterned fabric, so I strengthened the line with silk-ribbon roses and beading. Adding beadwork to the lace attracts the eye to the beads first, as the beads are a contrast of texture. They shine and sparkle, adding variety and interest without too much bling. Everyone has a different level of what is defined as "too much," and you will find yours as you experiment.

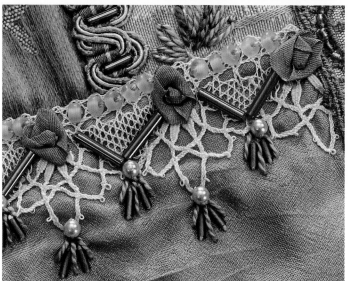

I have echoed the pattern of this lace. It looks like a complex treatment, but it is simply a line of pink seed beads along the top and long bugle beads stitched in a V formation, with fargo roses placed at the peaks. The bottom of the lace was secured with straight stitches and smaller bugle beads that echo the V-like formation of the large pink bugle beads. In the middle of this is a small bead. The descriptions sound complicated, but in echoing the V shape, repetition is setting up a pattern.

Patterning is a very powerful method of creating a pleasant visual experience. Crazy quilting as a style has foundation pieces of fabric made of a feast of materials, which breaks any notion of pattern, so providing little areas of visual respite in the form of predictable patterns creates a moment of visual pleasure for your viewer. In other words, pattern creates relief.

A line of lace can also echo a theme on a block. Here I emphasized the flower pattern by adding straight stitches and a bead to the middle of each motif. At the base of the lace, I added some novelty beads that are shaped like butterflies. To create visual interest once again, I used repetition along a seam. In this one little area of the block there are three repeats. The repeated lace pattern of flowers is emphasized with a bead in the middle of each flower. The embroidered scallops are repeated and emphasized with another repeated pattern created by the butterfly beads.

Add beads in line along the outer edge of a scallop. Straight stitches along the top echo the fan pattern seen in the seam. This simple decoration means that even the most novice embroiderer can decorate the seam.

Seed beads can be used to secure the edge of lace. The novelty heart-shaped beads here are inverted to echo the edge.

You can "grow" the width of a seam by using embroidery. Echo the pattern on the lace in stem stitch scallops using perle cotton #5. The spokes are straight stitches decorated with seed beads.

Don't forget to consider other types of lace, such as tatting. Echo the curves of the tatted lace with chain-stitched scallops. The scallops are not an exact repeat of the pattern, but they are a similar-shaped curve that is scaled slightly larger.

You can use lace in many different ways. Decorate pieces of tatting from the same length in different ways. A running stitch, woven using a thicker yarn, is used along the seam in this example. Then a fan of straight stitches with seed beads is placed at regular intervals.

This is an even easier seam embellishment. Secure the tatting to the block; then add beads in the middle of the loops.

You can also stitch right on top of lace. It deepens the visual texture and always surprises people when you don't stick to decorating the seams in a predictable way.

A simple floral spray ties areas together. Notice how the spray is not tightly on the seamline and how it spills over into the patches and over onto areas of lace. In doing so, it ties all pieces of lace together.

You can embellish lace in a simple manner or add as much complexity as you like, but I hope these few images have convinced you to add some lace to your block.

A wide range of small lace motifs is available on the market. These can be used along a seam or as a point of emphasis. It's all of the fun for a quarter of the work.

I often encounter beginners who are not confident about hand embroidering motifs on a block. For some, the combination of being new to both crazy quilting and embroidery means that they do not want to spend hours stitching a motif to find that it does not sit well compositionally on the block. Using lace motifs is an ideal, quick solution to this situation. You can learn crazy quilting before committing to developing hand embroidery skills. There is nothing wrong with doing this until you feel at ease investing the time in more complex styles of hand embroidery.

:: One of the easiest ways of producing a dramatic effect on your work is to use single-flower motifs to make a floral spray along a seam. Don't be fearful of spilling over into the patches on the block or embroidering over the lace. Layering like this can add dimension and texture.

:: If the block is already complex, use a lighter approach and secure the lace with just a few beads.

You can also use a lace motif as a point of emphasis. Using a carefully placed motif can solve compositional problems. If, for instance, a block looks too heavy on one side, add a lace motif to the other side. Baste the motifs to the block until you have made your final decision, and, when ready, secure them in place with a few small stitches. I mainly use beads to make the lace motif a feature.

:: A lace motif secured with beads

USING BRAIDS

There are many beautiful commercial braids and ribbons on the market. Since both are thin strips of decorative material, both function within a composition in a similar manner. They create thin lines, which can mean the eye slides quickly along them. Often, braids and ribbons move the eye a bit too quickly, but you can slow the viewer's experience down by adding texture and detail, so that the eye lingers longer in a particular area of a block. How do you add texture and detail? With the use of embroidery and beading, of course!

tip Commercial braids, ribbons, and laces come in a variety of widths. Try to have a mix of widths on the block. The same width of lace or braid on only a few seams can look too predictable. Vary the scale by placing a wide piece of lace against a thin braid to make it more interesting.

·······················**NOTE**·······················

See how the viewer's eye travels more quickly over braid and ribbon than it does over lace? I tried to slow the eye down with the details on the braid, but the eye still moves quickly along its length. Also look at the button cluster on the block. Normally I would not use quite so many buttons. The lace behind it is very old and I wanted to use it because it had sentimental value. It was torn, so I hid the problem with buttons. It made for an interesting area on the block where the viewer could linger for a moment before continuing.

∷ Seams covered with braid, lace, and ribbon

How can you use ribbons and braids to enhance your design? What does it look like on a real block? When piecing blocks, some people go to extraordinary lengths to avoid a long seam. I don't see a long seam on a block as problem.

This is an example of a block with a long seam. It runs from middle left to top right. Not only is this seam long, but a second seam is running almost parallel with it. (I have marked these two lines on the diagram with a blue dashed line.) Some would feel that the eye travels too quickly along the line and shoots off the edge of the block. Notice how I have marked in red where I used a line of buttons set against wide lace to create my usual journey for the eye zigzagging over that area of the block. The viewer is so busy looking at the lace, beads, and buttons that they don't really sit much on the long seam.

Braids are quick and easy to decorate. You do not need to be an expert embroiderer to take advantage of them. This braid was secured to the block with some very small stitches using regular machine sewing thread. Then straight stitches and seed beads were added to the dips in the scallops.

This yellow braid has a white thread laced through the lock-stitching along the edge, creating a zigzag line. That pattern was echoed in embroidery, creating a repeat of the zigzag line in straight stitches. I decorated the line with detached chain stitches, seed beads, and novelty beads. These stitches are not difficult. The trick is to pick out an element in the braid (such as the zigzag line), repeat it, and decorate it.

Using repetition as an element of your design becomes very natural once you start. Above, bugle beads emphasize the red bands that run across the braid and add further decoration by arranging detached chain stitches at right angles to the braid. These were worked in perle cotton #5. The novelty beads were added last.

You don't have to work both sides of the braid. In this case, I was happily adding arrangements of quarter-daisies in detached chain stitches when I decided I did not want to embroider over the lace below. So I stopped halfway along the line. There are no rules in crazy quilting.

You do not have to overload every seam with heavy embellishment. I beaded just the braid, but look at the embellishment on the lace. It is far more complex. The braid sits in contrast to the lace, but they also echo each other and are tied together visually by using similar colors. Different colors would not have married well.

Lace and braid work together. This braid was decorated with quarter-daisies of detached chain stitches and beads. The lace has a novelty bead added at regular intervals along the line. Since both are of a similar width, an added embroidered scallop makes the lace appear wider than the braid.

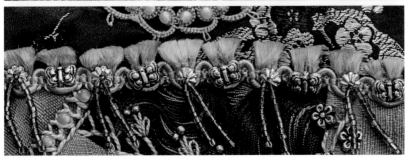

Some braids are just plain quirky. This one has fuzzy tufts. I added novelty beads in the shape of butterflies at every second tuft. The braid had so much personality that bead tassels were in order!

USING RIBBONS

Ribbons are delightful to use in crazy quilting. You can stitch them along a seam or explore the wonderful world of ribbon work and ribbon embroidery.

Braids and ribbons will affect a composition in a similar way, since the eye slides quickly along the line they create. Much of what I have said about braids applies to ribbons, too (refer to Using Braids, page 48).

The pink woven ribbon inspired the color scheme and the flower spray on this block. Small lace flowers echo the pattern woven into the ribbon. Along the edge of the ribbon, detached chain and straight stitches are used in almost an identical manner as a floral spray to tie the block together. In the case of this block, I kept the spray light with such a large spray of flowers. A heavily embroidered and beaded spray would have dominated the area, as the spray covers half the block.

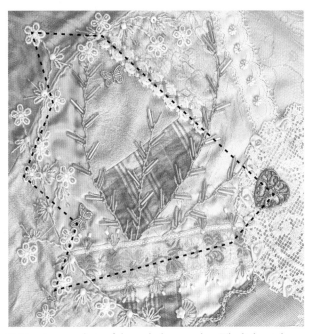

Here is an analysis of the path the eye takes. The light pink braid at the top of the block was secured with a zigzag chain stitch that "points" to the heart charm. The line created by the braid is being reinforced by the heart charm, which is a point of interest. I placed the doily on the right side of the block to prevent the eye from traveling along the woven ribbon and right off the block. The curved cup of feather stitches decorated with bugle beads on the left side of the block draws attention away from the edges and keeps the eye wandering over the block.

Embroidery was added along the edges of this ribbon. I used perle cotton #8 thread to work quarter-daisies of detached chain stitches.

This ribbon was secured to the block with bugle and seed beads. It only needed a light touch of beads to enhance the pattern since it is such a beautiful ribbon.

In this case I wanted a dramatic statement! Many ribbons can be used in crazy quilting, even if they are wide. This ribbon was 1½″ (3.8 cm) wide, so a button cluster could be layered on top of it without the buttons taking over.

You can also cover a seam with couched ribbon. Satin ribbons are readily available and come in a full color range in a number of widths, so it is easy to find the right width and color to match your project. Here, satin ribbon was secured with a line of herringbone stitches using perle cotton #5. It was then laced with a fine black knitting yarn with gold flecks in it, providing a visual lift to the stitches. Detached chain stitches and seed beads were added.

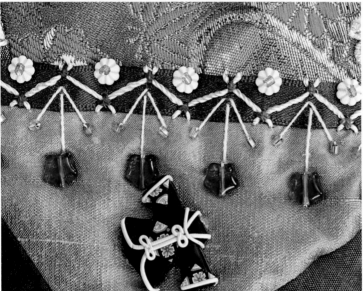

Satin ribbon is couched with a herringbone stitch using perle cotton #5. The herringbone stitches were secured with small blue cross-stitches using perle cotton #8 before adding straight stitches and novelty beads.

Velvet ribbons come in a variety of widths and colors and add a luxurious feel and richness to a block. A line of bullion buds was worked down the middle of this ribbon.

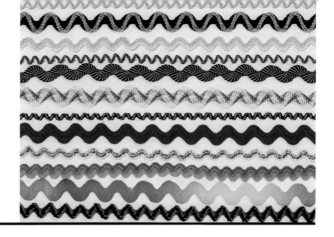

USING RICKRACK

Rickrack is available in numerous sizes, colors, and textures, and it is economical. You do not need to be an expert embroiderer to include it on your block, and rickrack is a quick way to add movement.

Rickrack can be couched to a block using a herringbone, chevron, or Cretan stitch, or, as in this example, a zigzag chain stitch. This line did not have much contrast against the foundation fabric, so chain-stitch loops and detached chain stitches were added.

A zigzag chain stitch secures the rickrack, with small novelty beads sewn to the hills and valleys. Groups of four small beads stitched in a straight line widen the line and create variety.

The rickrack was secured with sets of four seed beads arranged in a line. Three detached chain stitches couch the rickrack to the block. It is enjoyable to think up new ways to use stitches and beads in the tradition of innovation. These personal touches allow each crazy quilter to develop a style that is unique to their hand.

This rickrack has a pattern that looks like a running stitch, so I left it alone and decorated the edges with fargo roses, straight stitches, and detached chain stitches worked in a variegated perle cotton #5. The change of color along the length of the thread was all that was needed to add variety.

This looks more complex but is really very simple. The rickrack was secured with zigzag chain stitches. Detached chain stitches in perle cotton #5 were added on the second pass. Straight stitches worked in metallic sewing machine thread were added before the seed beads. Since the embroidery and beading is closely spaced, the seam looks more heavily embellished. It is the density of the stitches that make it feel rich, but "beginner" stitches were was used to achieve the effect.

USING DOILIES AND HANKIES

If you want to include doilies and hankies in a project, add them at the piecing stage, since these items not only effect the composition but can set the mood of the block. Doilies and hankies are often associated with relatives. So strong are the associations that if you buy doilies from secondhand shops to include in your crazy quilting projects, viewers will be curious to know if they came from a family member.

tip Both doilies and hankies are often made of cotton, which means they accept dye very easily. Simple commercial dyes, such as Rit, will dye lace, ribbons, braids, doilies, hankies, and even some buttons. The dye pot can really add a fun factor to crazy quilting.

∷ A hand-dyed crochet doily on a block

Doilies and hankies can be quite large on a block and therefore dominate. Even if you cut them into quarters, they can take over in some situations and attract too much attention in the quilt.

If you want to use doilies and hankies on a large project, such as a quilt, you can solve this challenge by designing a quilt where the blocks that feature doilies and hankies are part of the set of the quilt. For instance, you could create a quilt with a central medallion of blocks that feature doilies and hankies, with a border of blocks that feature doilies and hankies, or with just corner blocks that feature doilies and hankies. The trick is to be consistent.

Consider the scale of the doily or hankie and the embroidery and embellishment on top. The size of these elements can throw off the design, so when you use these, consider the impact they will have on the composition of the block. If you plunk a doily down on a block, it will stick out. Think of it as part of a layer in the embellishment process, and decorate it as you would your seams or patches.

∷ The part of the doily used in the middle of this block is cut down, so other elements on the block can counterbalance it. The bow and vintage dark pink lace both draw the eye away. As a general rule of thumb, I cut the doily or hankie smaller than the largest fabric patch on the block.

Another trick is to scale up everything else on the block. The band of lace in the bottom right corner is much larger than the doily. Or place points of emphasis away from the doily. On this block, both the button cluster and the lace butterfly motif draw the viewer's eye away from the doily, making it less noticeable.

This doily is counterbalanced with a large spray of embroidered flowers, which also moves the eye around the block. The block is ideal to use in the bottom left-hand corner of a quilt, because it would move the eye not just around the block but also up toward the middle of the quilt.

I would place this block at the bottom center of a quilt because there is a strong sweep upwards away from the doily. This deflects the eye away from the doily but also can be used to point the eye toward the middle of the quilt. Although the lines of embroidery form a strong cuplike shape, the eye is deflected back into the block with the line of herringbone stitches at the top left and the seam covered with embellished tatting at the top right. In a block like this, the viewer's eye is able to roam over the block, then wander elsewhere over the quilt surface.

There are many inventive ways to embellish doilies and hankies. The first is very simple; those new to crazy quilting can do it because the seam is covered with braid and novelty buttons. Along one edge, scallops were worked in a stem stitch using perle cotton #5. Notice how the stitched scallops echo the scallops on the edge of the doily and in the braid.

This is the edge of a serviette. The edge was defined with stem and chain stitches using perle cotton #8. Straight stitches, pearls, and seed beads were then added. These stitches are easy to work, which means they are a good choice for inexperienced embroiderers.

This simple treatment is very effective. Two straight stitches and two detached chain stitches hug a bead using perle cotton #5. These stitches and techniques are considered basic surface stitches, but they are ideal for crazy quilting because they are so versatile.

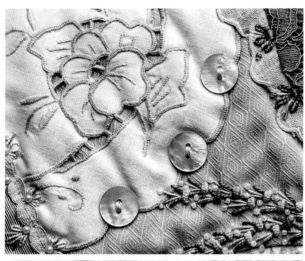

You do not even need embroidery. All you need to do is stitch on a button. The three buttons form a line around the edge where the eye moves effortlessly along.

Detached chain stitches and bullion knots with loops of seed beads echo the edge of the doily.

Hankies often have a corner of lace that can be embroidered or beaded. Sometimes all you need to do is to add a few beads. A hankie corner was secured to the block with tiny running stitches made along the edge using regular white sewing machine thread; then beads were added. If lace doilies or hankies are flapping about and getting in the way, just secure them with a few stitches.

Beading and buttons were used to secure the corner of the hankie. Seed beads were used to outline the main line of embroidery, but you could use a stem stitch or chain stitch instead. Don't be afraid to use buttons in your crazy quilting because they attract attention. They can create a point of emphasis and are quick and easy to apply. Because these buttons were in the shape of flowers, I added some leaf ribbon stitches and the decoration was done.

Adding Prairie Points

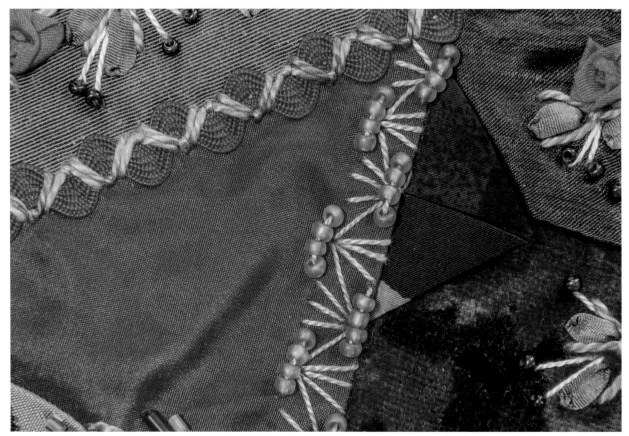

∷ Prairie points used on a crazy quilt seam

Prairie points used in crazy quilting are a fun surprise for your viewer. They are a modern touch that can be made out of ribbon or scraps of fabric. I add prairie points at the piecing stage.

tip Making prairie points from the same fabric as a patch used on the opposite side of the block can help tie the block together.

∷ Prairie points are little triangles, which means their shape can influence the composition because they behave as little arrows. They can be used to point to areas you want the viewer to see.

MAKING PRAIRIE POINTS

If you are making prairie points from fabric scraps, cut the squares twice as large as the finished point plus ¼″ (0.6 cm).

1. For a 1″ (2.5 cm) prairie point, cut a square of fabric 2¼″ × 2¼″ (5.7 cm × 5.7 cm).

2. Fold the square in half horizontally and press.

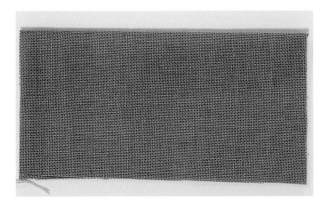

3. Fold the upper right corner down and bring the pressed edge to the center, creating a fold at a 45° angle. Press.

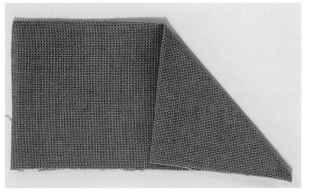

4. Fold the left corner down to meet the center pressed edge, and press the 45° fold.

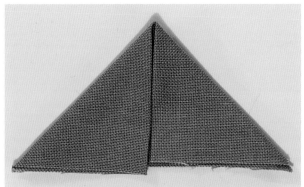

You can make small prairie points out of ribbon. They are easy to make and a great way of using up small scraps. Using a small piece of ribbon—about 2″ (5.1 cm) long—follow Steps 3 and 4 above. If the ribbon is slippery, I baste the prairie point in place before sewing the base of the prairie point in the seam of the block. After the prairie point is securely stitched into the seam, trim any leftover ribbon from the base.

Your stitching can echo the shape of the prairie point. In this example, the triangular nature of the prairie point is echoed along the seam by creating stitches of a similar shape. I used detached chain stitches worked in a zigzag line and then threaded a rayon ribbon floss under each stitch to emphasize the line. While I had that floss in the needle, I added three straight stitches to the tip of the prairie point before working straight stitches in a fan-like formation. I added more straight stitches to the tip of the prairie point before working more straight stitches using gold metallic thread.

I like turning prairie points into little pockets. I delight in watching people discover them, and usually they cannot resist poking their finger in it! In this example, I used a buttonhole stitch along the side of the point. I worked it in perle cotton #8 and then added a few seed beads.

When using prairie points along the seam, use the same color embroidery thread to embellish both the seam and prairie point. This ties the two together because both the shape and color are repeated.

You can echo such elements as fabric, color, stitch, stitch shape, ribbon, lace, and so forth. Repetition is a powerful technique to keep in your toolbox. Pull it out and use it when a block does not look quite right.

I hope this section has given you a few ideas to use while piecing your block. All these extra embellishments are added as I piece. Once I have the block pieced, I embroider the seams, which you will learn about in the next section.

part four
Starting to Stitch

After you have pieced your crazy quilt project, the next step is to embroider the seams. The key stitches I use in crazy quilting projects are the buttonhole, chevron, Cretan, feather, herringbone, chain, stem, fly, and straight stitches.

Couching is also an invaluable technique, because it is quick and simple and you can incorporate heavy-weight novelty yarns and threads into your block. It is also worth learning how to do French knots and bullion knots, because both of these stitches enable you to produce interesting areas of decorative texture. These stitches also lend themselves to working floral designs. There are hundreds of surface embroidery stitches that are fun to explore and experiment with, but these basic stitches are really all you need to get started.

You can experiment and explore stitches and techniques using numerous materials, such as lace, braid, buttons, beads, and doodads, which means crazy quilting is always fun and inspiring.

Starting and Finishing

In crazy quilting it is perfectly acceptable to use a knot at the back of the block. This is easy and what most people do, because with a crazy quilt project, the back of the work is covered. If the project is a quilt or wallhanging, it is backed. If it is a bag or purse, it is lined. Often a little batting is used between the top and lining. This means that knots cannot be seen or felt.

When you finish a seam, take the thread to the back of the work and loop it under the previous stitch a couple of times to knot it off. Or you can do a few small back-stitches to secure the thread.

tip If your thread gets twisted and knotted as you stitch, turn your work upside down and drop the threaded needle. Let it hang freely until it unwinds.

Thread

Crazy quilting opens the door to the wonderful contemporary needlework threads that are on the market. Metallic threads, silks, cottons, and ribbons can all be used in crazy quilting.

Many people start crazy quilting with stranded cotton floss, but this type of thread is not really designed for surface embroidery. These multi-stranded threads are wonderful for cross-stitch, but often stitches worked on a block with floss will sit flat against the fabric instead of sitting proud. If you are embroidering on a fabric that has a little texture (such as velvet) or has a shine (such as satin), a thread with a twist will sit a little higher and be more noticeable. I always recommend using either perle cotton #5 or #8. You can buy them by the skein or by the ball.

There are hundreds of different commercial threads that you can use. I am not exaggerating. I love the variegated hand-dyed threads, and I constantly experiment with threads that contain bamboo, rayon, and Tencel.

Since you can work many styles of embroidery on your crazy quilting projects, you can use silk thread for silk ribbon embroidery. I like silk buttonhole twist, but there are many types of silk thread. Silk is the queen of threads, and once you've used it, addiction can become a problem.

tip Some of the novelty and synthetic threads can be difficult to sew with but are worth the patience, because they add a lovely texture and sheen to your work. The trick is to use shorter lengths of thread. Threads should be cut the same length as the distance between the tip of your thumb and elbow. This is the maximum "pull" of your arm. You will have fewer knots because there are fewer loops created during the stitching process with a shorter thread.

Metallic threads are available in different weights and textures and can add sparkle to your work. There are times when metallic thread is definitely called for, such as on crazy quilted Christmas decorations. Some of my favorite metallics are Kreinik Fine #8 Braid threads that come in various colors. DMC makes metallic silver and gold threads that are available on 43.7-yard (40 m) spools.

When buying metallic threads, look carefully at the thread to see if the metallic fiber is twisted together. Avoid the reels that are marked as "blending" threads, as these filaments are meant to be used with a second thread. They are not strong enough to be used on their own.

Chenille was very popular in Victorian crazy quilts. It is a fuzzy velvety thread that has a pile spun into the core. You can stitch with cotton and silk chenilles because they have a tightly wound core that will stand up to being pulled through the fabric. However, the vast majority of the synthetic and cheaper chenille threads have a core of a looser twist. This means you have to couch them to your block rather than actually stitching with them.

Wool threads are normally used in crewel embroidery, but I add them to crazy quilting, too. Paternayan Persian

wool is a good choice. Novelty and knitting yarns can also be used for lacing, threading, and couching to your block.

Rayon ribbon floss looks like a small thin ribbon of silk but is actually made of rayon. It has a pliable structure, which means it is less likely to twist and is easy to stitch with.

tip Rayon threads can be particularly tricky to use. I cut a short length of thread and dampen it to remove kinks, running it across a damp sponge, before I stitch. I found this to be the most effective way of using rayon.

Silk ribbons vary greatly in width. The most common are 2 mm, 4 mm, 7 mm, and 13 mm widths. I use 4 mm and 7 mm the most.

THREAD FOR BEADING

Nymo and Silamide are the most commonly used threads for beading. I have used both. I have also used regular sewing cotton, particularly when I first started crazy quilting, and the beads are still on the quilts. I particularly use regular sewing cotton if the color matches better.

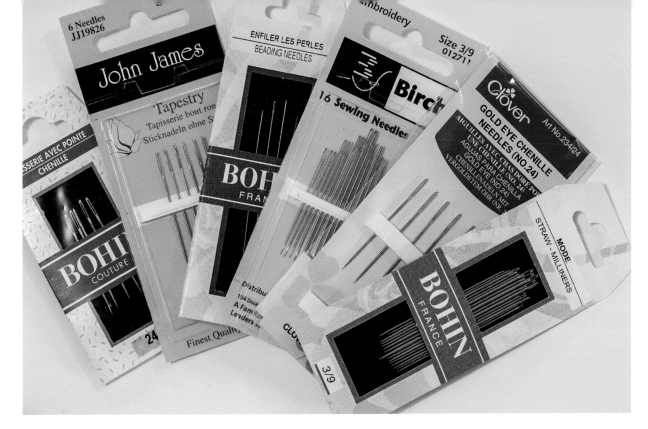

Needles

One of the attractions of crazy quilting is that you can use many types of threads. When using such a wide variety of threads, however, you need to think about the fabric and what needle to use. Choose a thread that is suitable for that fabric; then choose your needle. Choosing the correct needle means the thread can go through the eye with reasonable ease but the eye is not so large as to cause the thread to rub and fray as you stitch. Check to see if the needle slides through the fabric easily; a fabric with a tight weave will need a fine needle, whereas a fabric that has a looser weave will be able to take a larger needle and, as a result, thicker threads.

tip Needle sizing can confuse some people. Just remember the larger number, the thinner the needle.

CREWEL OR EMBROIDERY NEEDLES

Because you will be using a variety of embroidery threads, you will need a mix of needle sizes to accommodate them. Embroidery or crewel needles have a sharp point with a long eye. The long eye allows for a range of embroidery threads, making them ideal for most types of surface embroidery. You can purchase embroidery needles in packets that have a range of sizes. I find I mostly use sizes 6, 7, and 8, but it is good to find what you are comfortable with, so mixed size packets are good when you start crazy quilting. As you do more stitching, you will find you favor one size over another; you can buy those in single-size packets later.

STRAW OR MILLINERS NEEDLES

For stitches such as French knots and bullion knots, you will need a needle with an eye that does not bulge and is level with the shaft of the needle, such as a milliners needle. This type of needle is useful for any stitch that involves wrapping the thread around the needle multiple times and then pushing the wraps along the needle shaft. The wraps of working thread will slide over the eye of the needle and not be caught up. Stitches such as French knots and bullion knots are all easier to work with a milliners needle. They come in sizes 3–10, and I always have a range on hand so I can work these textured stitches in different types of thread.

TAPESTRY NEEDLES

Tapestry needles are short, blunt-tipped needles designed to take thick or multiple strands of cotton or wool through their long eye. They come in sizes 18–28 and can be purchased in mixed-size packets. For the threaded and whipped stitches, use a blunt-ended tapestry needle to weave a second thread through the foundation stitches to avoid splitting the foundation row during the lacing.

Tapestry Needles and Beading

With some stitches, you can bead as you go if you use the right needle. If you use a tapestry #26 needle, the eye is long, which means you can use either perle cotton #5 or #8. However, the needle itself is thin, which means you can add a seed bead to your working thread as you stitch. This technique adds tremendous versatility to many surface embroidery stitches.

CHENILLE NEEDLES

Chenille needles have a sharp point, a bit like crewel needles, but they are thicker and longer. This means they have larger eyes that enable you to use a heavier thread. They are used with silk ribbon embroidery. You need a needle that makes a fair-sized hole when it pierces the foundation fabric, allowing the ribbon to glide through. If the hole is too small, the ribbon will stress and fray.

Chenille needles are commonly available in sizes 13–26 and can be purchased in mixed packets. For silk ribbon embroidery, I generally recommend the following:

- Chenille #24 needle for 2 mm ribbon

- Chenille #22 or #24 needle for 4 mm ribbon (Choose what feels best to you.)

- Chenille #20 or #22 chenille needle for 7 mm ribbon

BEADING NEEDLES

Beading needles are long, thin, and fine enough to go through a seed bead. They can be difficult to thread because of this. Using a needle threader solves this problem. Beading needles come in sizes 10–15 and also come in mixed packets.

Silk Ribbon Embroidery

Ribbon work and silk ribbon embroidery have delighted stitchers since the Victorian era. It is a remarkably easy yet impressive form of stitching. Many beginners feel intimidated by it because it looks so difficult, yet it is not. Silk ribbon embroidery produces a spray of flowers in just a bit of time.

The main thing with silk ribbon embroidery is to use actual silk. Many beginners seek to economize and use satin ribbon. Satin does not fold and drape the same way as silk. I am not a fiber snob; when I can substitute something cheaper, I will. But in the case of silk ribbon embroidery, you really do have buy silk ribbon.

The other tip I have for beginners is to keep the ribbon loose. Don't use too much tension as you stitch. Let the stitches be full and flop about a bit, and the softness of the silk will do most of the work for you.

Make sure the ribbon is crease free. Wind the ribbon around something to prevent creases. Just about anything will do. The cardboard cylinders from food wrap or empty plastic thread spools work well.

HOW TO LOCK YOUR RIBBON

Silk ribbon can slip and slide in a needle eye, and in doing so can fray. To prevent this, you need to "lock" the ribbon.

1. Cut the ribbon on an angle and thread it through the eye of the needle.

2. Place the point of the needle about ⅝″ (7 mm) from the end of the ribbon closest to the needle. I know it sounds crazy, but push the needle all the way through the end of the ribbon.

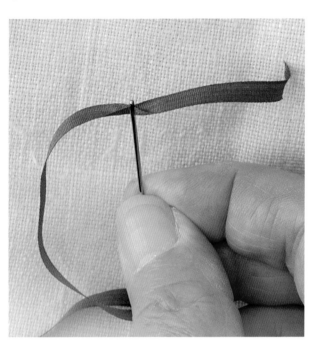

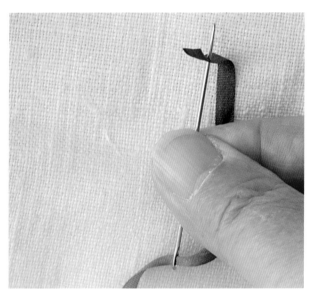

3. Pull the needle through until a knot forms at the eye. This locks the ribbon.

4. The ribbon is now locked in the needle!

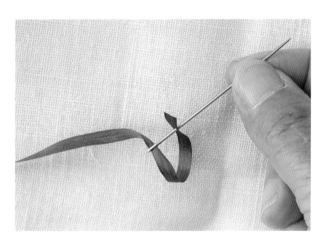

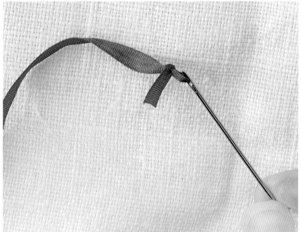

Beads

There is a huge range of beads on the market. Most of the modestly sized beads are suitable for crazy quilting. When I am starting a new project, I select my beads as I piece my block. I make some "bead soup," which is a mix of seed beads, bugle beads, sequins, and novelty beads. I keep them in a container that lives with my project. I choose beads from the dominant color, and I always include a few beads from the complementary colors, in addition to a few gold and silver metal beads.

If you use plastic beads and touch them with an iron, they will melt! For that reason, many beaders insist on glass beads. However, plastic beads are lighter than glass. If you are making a large quilt to hang on a wall, using plastic beads will mean that the finished quilt's weight will be lighter than if you had used glass beads.

SEED BEADS

Seed beads are small beads that are usually made from glass. With bead sizes, the larger the number, the smaller the bead. For beading embroidery stitches, use a tapestry #26 needle. The eye of a tapestry needle is long and you can thread perle cotton #5 or #8 through the long eye. The needle itself is thin, which means you can add a bead to your working thread as you stitch.

For simply attaching beads to your crazy quilt projects, a #10 needle will easily fit through a size 11 seed bead. Czech and Japanese seed beads are the most common and are available in a wide range of sizes and finishes. The most common size for seed beads is 11, but sizes 10–15 can be found quite easily.

BUGLE BEADS

Bugles are long tube-shaped beads of cut glass. They vary in length and finish and are sized by numbers, with 1 being the smallest and 2 being the most common. Pressed glass or novelty beads are glass beads made in shapes such as flowers and leaves.

Marking Your Fabric

Use a quilter's pencil or one of the commercial pens that are designed to disappear to mark the grid on the fabric. What works on one type of fabric might not work on another, so have a selection of pens and pencils designed for quilters and needleworkers. These can be found in stores that specialize in needlework and quilting.

If the fabric is dark, use a white quilter's pencil or dressmaker's white chalk pencil. If the fabric is light, use a lead pencil or one of the blue or purple pens that are available on the market.

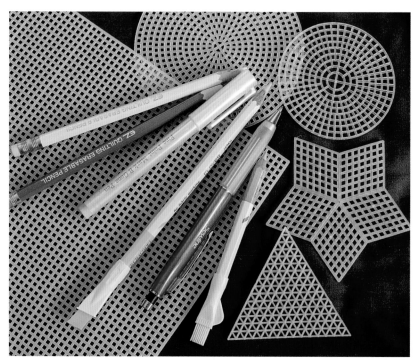

:: Plastic canvas and various marking pens and pencils

If you use the blue and purple quilter's pens, ironing the piece will set the pen marks. Also, marks made by some of the blue and purple pens have been known to reappear. With embroidery, you are often stitching over the lines that you mark; so if the marks do reappear, they will be hidden by your stitching. If the stitch is open, as is the case with herringbone, buttonhole, Cretan, chevron, or straight stitches, mark their base and height with small dots. The dots will not seen because the thread of the stitch will hide them.

One problem with disappearing-ink pens is, if you don't stitch the seam within a day or two, the line will disappear. If you put your block marked with the disappearing pen in a zip-top bag, it won't fade as fast. Do not store textiles in plastic bags long term; only do so while working on a block and only for a few days.

How do you keep your seam stitches straight? I use a plastic canvas grid to create a series of dots that will act as a guide for stitches. Plastic canvas is a lightweight plastic that can be purchased in craft or needlework stores in a number of different sizes and shapes. It is inexpensive, and you can cut it easily with scissors, so you can cut a small piece to tuck neatly into your sewing box. I use the most common size of plastic canvas grid, which is seven-count canvas mesh.

:: Lay plastic canvas against the seam, and mark dots where your needle should enter
:: and emerge from the fabric.

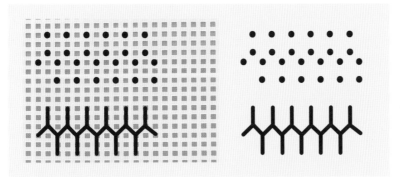

The dot pattern for the Cretan stitch; each dot indicates where the needle should be inserted in the fabric.

With the shaped version of plastic canvas, such a round disk, you can create fans and flowers. The star shape has a grid that creates V-shaped formations.

For many stitches in crazy quilting, you sew a line of stitches along a seam, then work a second row to decorate them further. The stitches you first sew are called *foundation stitches*. The foundation stitches include the herringbone, Cretan, chevron, buttonhole and feather stitch families, and stitches like the fly stitch. You can mark your foundation stitches using a canvas grid to easily work an even row.

Each foundation stitch has a different dot pattern, but once you get used to marking your seams like this, you will soon find the pattern of dots easy. Alongside directions on how to work foundation hand embroidery stitches, I have created grid patterns for people to use. Usually once you have done it a couple of times, it is not hard (refer to Stitches and Techniques, page 76).

USING TEMPLATES AS A GUIDE FOR STITCHES

Not all designs in crazy quilting have a base row of foundation stitches worked in a line along a seam. Some designs consist of things like floral sprays, shapes, or scallops that run along a seam or are used in small motifs on the patches of the block. For these designs, use stitches like the stem stitch or chain stitch, and use some form of template to keep the lines even.

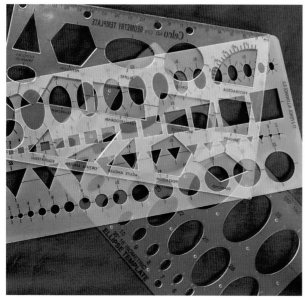

Mark a line of scallops along a seam, trace around a coin, or use commercial stencils created for graphic designers. You can also use scrapbooking stencils or cut your own templates from quilter's plastic or cardboard.

I have designed sets of templates for use with crazy quilting. With them you can create hundreds of different patterns to embroider on your crazy quilt projects. They are easy to use and clear, so you can position them easily on your block. My crazy quilt templates are also compact in your sewing box. They are available on my website (pintangle.com).

Position the template. Holding it firmly with one hand so it does not shift, use a quilter's pencil to trace along the edge of the template and create the pattern.

Decorating Your Seams and Designing Stitches

Many crazy quilters are intimidated when it comes to embellishing seams because the process looks so complex. Crazy quilt seams look complicated because people see the finished seams. What they don't see is that the seams have been built layer upon layer using a combination of stitches and techniques.

What do I mean by this? I mean that you start with a basic foundation row with a stitch such as herringbone. After you stitch a line of herringbone, for example, you add another line of stitches to it. You might decide to add two detached chain stitches tucked between each fork, then maybe a straight stitch that you can top with a little bead. With each element you add, the visual complexity increases.

tip If you get stuck on stitching ideas, photograph your unembellished block and print out a few copies. Sketch possible stitch combinations. Since you are not yet stitching, the pressure is off and your ideas will start to flow. You will be inspired by one or two ideas and think to yourself, "I want to do that!" At that point, put down your pencil, pick up your needle, and start to sew.

A misconception that stitchers have is that you need to know lots of stitches to do crazy quilting. This really is not the case. I suggest that you master three or four foundation stitches and the stem or chain stitch, since they are useful for making lines. Then master a few of the stitches I call *motif stitches*. I call them this because you arrange them in little motifs to decorate a seam or add them to a patch as a motif in their own right. You will be kept busy for years if you learn these stitches and work them in combination. However, once you have mastered these stitches, the bug has bitten and it is time to explore more of the many surface stitches.

Combining stitches is one way to make crazy quilting unique, fun, and surprising. No two people combine stitches the same way. The way to use stitches is very much up to personal taste, skill level, thread choice, color choice, what you have on hand, and how inventive you are. When you first start crazy quilting, you try one thing and then another, gradually developing confidence to become more inventive. In doing so, you are also developing your own approach and style.

Combining Stitches

When combining stitches, think about contrasting elements such as threads, color, or scale. Make your seams a little more interesting by varying the thread. A single line of herringbone stitch is nice, but treat it as the starting point and do something else with it, too. Create interest with a little contrast.

tips

- Vary the thickness and type of thread for a contrast of texture.

- Use different colors that contrast with your fabric and other stitches.

- Change the spacing and work the stitches far apart or close together, or overlap and stack stitches.

- Change the size and scale of your stitches.

- Repeat or echo the shape of your stitches.

- Change the direction and angle of your stitches to create movement.

When stitching, think about interesting visual contrasts you can share with your viewer. I started with a row of herringbone, which is an angular stitch. I contrasted that angular feel by lacing the line of stitching with a fine metallic cord. The curve of the lacing sets up an interesting contrast particularly, since this softness is enhanced with the soft silk ribbon buds. The softness of the buds is contrasted with the hard metal beads that are placed in between them.

Contrast your threads with your background fabric.

Don't limit yourself to experimenting with different threads. Use different threads on the same seam decoration. Use different colors on the same seam, or use a variegated or space-dyed thread, so the color changes as you stitch the seam. Also try using thicker and thinner threads or a thread that has a greater sheen than the others. These small contrasts add interest.

Look at the fabric you are embroidering. Does it have a sheen? If so, what does a thread that is dull look like against it? Are you stitching on cotton? What does a thread with a sheen look like? How would a metallic look?

When you think in terms of color contrast, remember your color wheel and color theory (see Value: Tints, Tones, and Shades, page 25). Don't forget that you can have a cool/warm color contrast on a seam or select a complementary color.

Start with a line of feather stitches worked in perle cotton. Then add burnt gold bugle beads to create a cool/warm color contrast. It is not a bold or bright visual jump, but it is a contrast.

Create color contrast on a seam. I used greens, which are set next to a bone/cream-toned fabric. On the seam, I have contrasted the green with an orange shade.

If you are creating a monochromatic block, think about both the texture and color of your thread. You will need some sort of contrast to make the embroidery interesting. The contrast between fabric and embroidery might be subtle, but in order to be seen and to be interesting, the thread may be a slightly different shade or it may have a different sheen when set against the fabric.

Often, the contrast is not thread but can be a bead. Beads are wonderful for lifting a seam, because they are bright and glittery and they attract the viewer's eye. Then the viewer goes on to notice other things about the seam or block.

Think about the shape of your stitches. Some combinations of stitches form shapes. Some are square, some form circles, and some are triangular. Think about working similar shapes along a seam.

Use a combination of detached chain stitches, straight stitches, and beads repeated along the seam. The two straight stitches are in a V formation. When I looked at the shape they created, I inverted that V shape and used a stem stitch to define it. Along the seam the shapes are similar, yet different enough to create an interesting contrast.

I echoed the shape of the half–buttonhole wheels with scalloped lines worked in chain stitches. The buttonhole wheels also echo the curves on the edge of the braid. These stitches are not difficult to work, and when combined, they make an interesting seam embellishment.

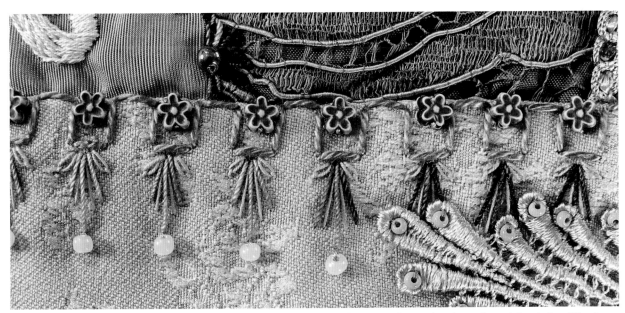

You can also contrast the shape of a row of stitches. This battlement brick pattern id created with simple straight stitches. The shape is a square, box-like line of stitches that acts as a foundation row. I have contrasted this with groups of splayed angular stitches. We can see other small contrasts, such as the contrast of texture with the flower bead at the base line and the seed bead at the top. Also, there is the contrast of color. None of these contrasts are dramatic, but they all combine to make an interesting decorative seam.

part five
Stitches and Techniques

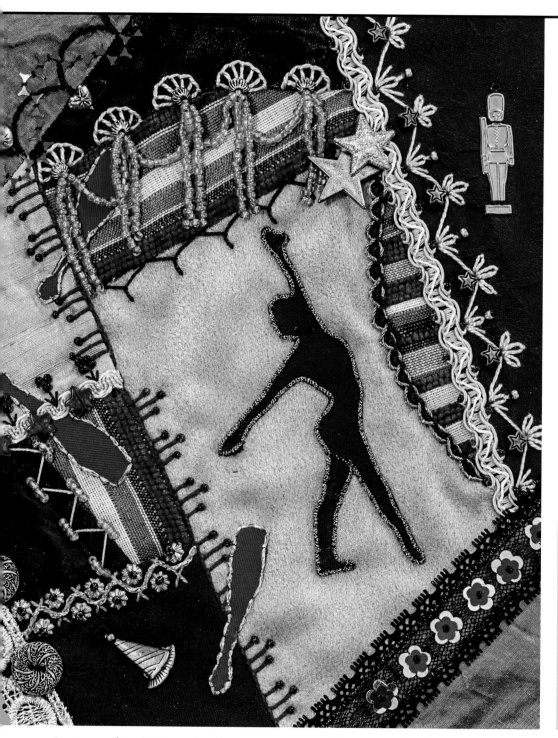

The first section covers the main surface embroidery stitches that are used as foundation rows on seams. This section is followed by linear stitches that are mainly used for outlining motifs, further decorating foundation rows or as vines and stems in floral sprays. The stitches in the last group are ideal to use as single unit motifs.

As your hand embroidery skills develop, you may want explore other surface embroidery stitches, combining and adapting them in inventive ways to create your own style. This keeps crazy quilting interesting, fun, and a delight to sit down to.

> **NOTE**
>
> Instructional stitch images on the following pages are labeled as:
>
> **R** Right-handed
>
> **L** Left-handed

Beginners often think that in order to master crazy quilting you need to know many embroidery stitches, and it comes as surprise that you need only a handful of stitches. In crazy quilting, you lay down a foundation of embroidery that is then decorated in a variety of ways. This chapter follows the process used to build a decorated crazy quilt seam.

Foundation Stitches

Buttonhole Stitch

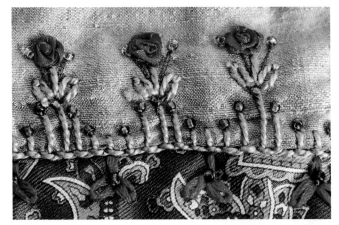

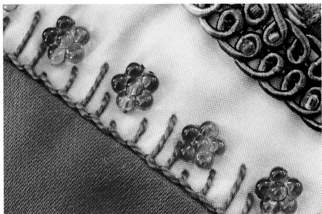

The buttonhole stitch, also known as the *blanket stitch*, is a classic surface embroidery stitch that is used as a foundation line on crazy quilt seams. It is quick and easy to work, will hold a curve, and looks great with beads added. Buttonhole has many adaptable variations.

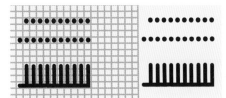

The dot pattern for the basic buttonhole stitch, using seven-count plastic canvas as a guide (refer to Marking Your Fabric, page 68). The buttonhole stitch is worked along two imaginary horizontal lines.

1. Bring the thread up from the back of the fabric on the lower imaginary line.

2. Insert the needle on the upper imaginary line one stitch-width over, and come out straight down on the lower imaginary line, looping the working thread under the needle.

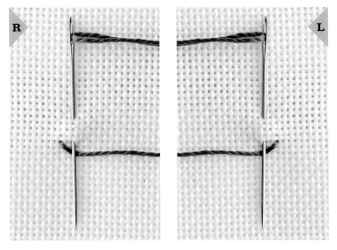

3. Pull the needle through the fabric to form a loop.

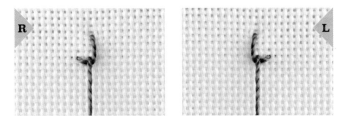

4. Repeat this process along the line.

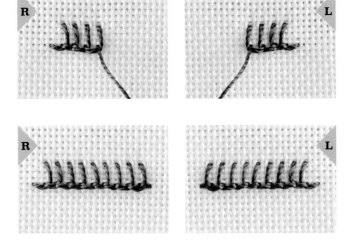

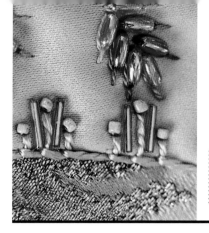

::: The fun feature of the buttonhole stitch is that you can vary the height of the "arms."

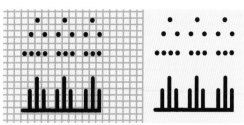

With this dot pattern, a basic buttonhole stitch becomes an interesting foundation row to build on.

Add small decorative elements such as detached chain stitches arranged as a little half-daisy.

Various flower motifs can be added on the second pass of stitching. For instance, you could use three detached chain and two straight stitches (a simple decoration), but any small motif stitch or beads and sequins can be used to decorate the line.

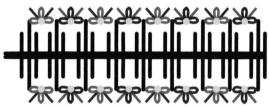

Working two rows back to back creates a thicker, more dramatic line. Using any stitch back to back is easy to do and is always worth experimenting with, because it offers more opportunities to decorate the simple stitches.

On the second pass, you can arrange the motifs in a zigzag pattern.

Change the placement of the little motifs.

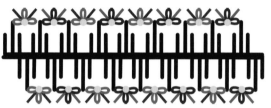

Offset the two lines of buttonhole stitches to create a different foundation pattern.

This pattern creates a wide seam decoration. One advantage to using such a wide seam embellishment is that it can balance another area of a block. If, for instance, you have a dominant point on the block, you can counterbalance it by using a wide seam elsewhere on the block. Or if you have bright color or dominant lace motif on the bottom left of a block, you can counterbalance this area with a wide decorative seam in the top right corner of the block.

Work two rows of buttonhole face to face and create a secondary pattern along the central line. This type of pattern is ideal to work over a wide satin ribbon. Baste the ribbon over the seam you want to decorate, and then embroider this pattern along the ribbon.

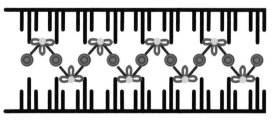

Add sequins to emphasize the zigzag motion.

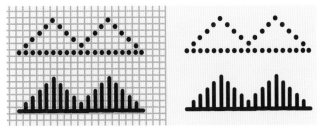

This dot pattern forms a triangular design by increasing the height of the stitch in steps.

Add motifs such as a simple arrangement of detached chain stitches and a French knot or bead.

Add partial buttonhole wheels. Adding, adapting, and swapping stitches creates what appears to be great variety. It is simple, as you are exchanging one stitch for another. You only need to know a few stitches that can be combined in different creative ways.

The same dot pattern worked back to back

Pull apart the two foundation rows and add another little motif down the centerline.

Work two staggered lines face to face; it is ideal to work over a wide satin ribbon.

Pull the two foundation rows further apart, and you have even more space to add something like a grape cluster made of French knots and a detached chain stitch.

This face-to-face arrangement creates a diamond area to fill with small motifs or even small buttons. In this case, look for the shape of the negative space that is created when you place the two foundation rows face to face. Once you see the shape, ask yourself the question, "What can I put there?" and use the space in a creative manner.

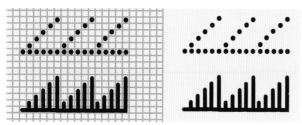

This dot pattern also gives some interesting design opportunities.

Add a line of decorative elements such as detached chain half-daisies.

Echo the pattern created by the line of foundation stitches with quarter–buttonhole wheels to form the flowers and detached chain stitches for the leaves. Add a bead or French knot to the base of each flower. Each stitch unit is angled to point in the same direction of the pattern created by the foundation stitches.

Place two foundation rows back to back. The pattern formed is a line of arrows. If ever you need to guide the viewer's eye back toward the center of a crazy quilt block, pointing these arrows inward toward the middle of block will help you achieve this. Use your seam embroidery not as decoration alone, but also when needed as a way to strengthen the composition of your block.

Work two lines of buttonhole stitch back to back, with one row flipped horizontally. You can emphasize the angle of the stitches by using a motif that echoes the angle.

If you work two foundation rows of buttonhole stitch back to back with a space between them, you create an area that allows you to add another little motif down the centerline.

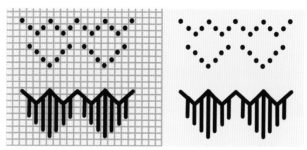

This dot pattern will open up even more decorative opportunities for a creative stitcher. With the buttonhole stitch, you can not only vary the length of the arms but also work the edge of the stitch in a zigzag.

This shows the addition of small motifs along the top of the foundation row. Here, small daisies are added using detached chain stitches.

Place small motifs in the negative space below the foundation row.

Work two rows back to back, but slightly apart, to allow space for a secondary row of small motifs.

Work two foundation rows face to face to create a diamond negative space along the middle line, which you can use for another motif. A third line of stitches turns a buttonhole foundation into an interesting seam embellishment.

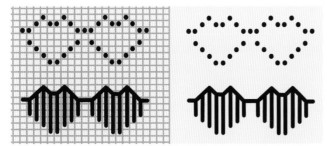

This dot pattern forms a line of hearts, which is particularly effective if you use a slightly thicker thread, such as perle cotton #5.

You can work the seam as it is or add motifs along the top.

This pattern looks good worked row upon row. It is very useful to fill an area.

Work this pattern back to back and fill the center with small stitches or sequin-and-bead motifs. People will look at it and wonder how you came up with the idea to adapt a basic buttonhole stitch so creatively.

Add small motifs to both the center and outside edges of this back-to-back pattern.

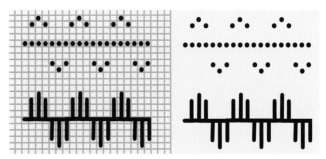

This dot pattern makes the stitches swing from side to side along the line. This is called *alternating buttonhole*, because usually you work some stitches on one side of the line before you work some on the other. I have a grid here of three stitches on each side of the line, but you can work more. You can vary the length of the arms, change the spacing, or even have three buttonhole stitches on one side and five on the other, creating an asymmetrical pattern for the foundation row.

One of the advantages to using an alternating buttonhole stitch is that it creates nicely shaped areas with enough space to create a secondary pattern on the second line of stitching.

Vary the height of the motif to develop a dynamic zigzag seam embellishment. Because the zigzag creates movement, it can add life to an area to move the viewer's eye around the block.

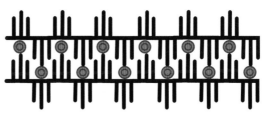

Here, the zigzag motion is created by a series of sequins that have been stitched between two foundation rows.

tip Complex seam decorations add interest and life to contemporary crazy quilting. They are also fun to do, and once you start, you will think of more and more ways to decorate them. Keep a little notebook beside you as you stitch, and write down your ideas as you think of them. You won't ever be stuck for ideas of what to stitch.

BEADED BUTTONHOLE STITCH

Nobody would expect the common buttonhole or blanket stitch to be so versatile, but it is! You can also bead the buttonhole stitch. You can substitute and adapt these patterns for any of the grid pattern in Buttonhole Stitch (pages 77). The possibilities are fun to explore and the combinations are endless.

Adding beads during the stitching process is a wonderful technique. The trick is to use a tapestry #26 needle. The eye of a tapestry needle is long, so you can thread it with embroidery floss. The needle is also thin, which means you can add a bead to your working thread as you stitch.

1. Bring the thread up from the back of the fabric on the lower imaginary line and work a regular buttonhole stitch.

2. Thread 3 or 4 seed beads or a bugle bead onto your working thread. Insert the needle on the upper line.

3. Loop the working thread under the needlepoint, keeping the beads to the right or left of the needle, as illustrated.

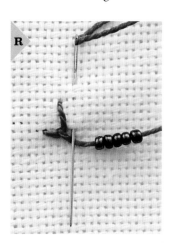 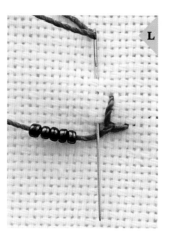

4. Pull the needle through the fabric to form a loop.

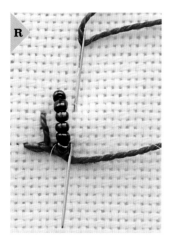 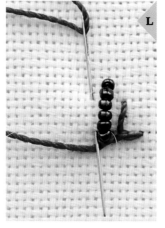

5. Work a regular buttonhole stitch and repeat this pattern of beading every second arm along the line.

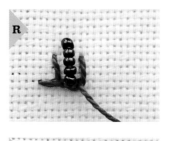 

Change where and when you thread a bead in order to create different patterns. You can apply this technique to all the buttonhole patterns (pages 77–81); there are dozens of varieties to explore. You can bead all the arms while varying the length and spacing of the arms, or you can bead some of the arms, setting up secondary patterns created by the beads.

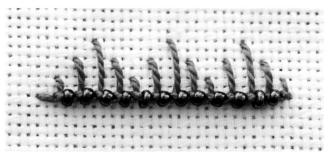

Bead the base line of the stitch. This is a great edging stitch for items such as small purses, needle books, and the like.

UP AND DOWN BUTTONHOLE STITCH

For the up and down buttonhole stitch, the arms are tied together with a small stitch. It makes a great addition to any crazy quilt block because you can vary the height and angle of the arms to create some very interesting patterns. Each stitch of the pair is separate step.

1. Bring the thread up from the back of the fabric on the lower imaginary line. Insert the needle on the upper imaginary line and come out on the lower imaginary line, looping the working thread under the needle. Pull the needle through the fabric to form a loop.

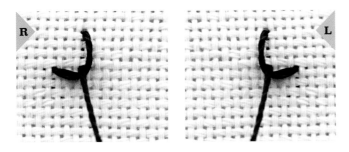

2. For the second part of the stitch (inverse stitch), insert the needle on the lower imaginary line and take a bite of the fabric, so that the tip of the needle is pointing upward at the upper imaginary line.

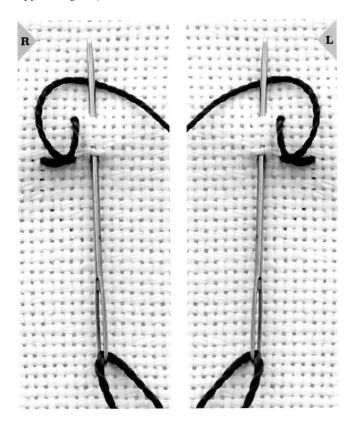

3. Wrap the working thread under the needle. As you pull the needle through, take your hand up in an arc and pull the thread toward you, instead of away from you, to form the loop that ties the 2 stitches together.

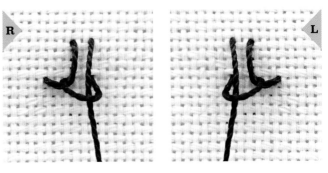

4. Pull taut.

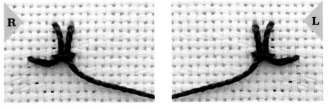

5. Work along the line, first with the regular buttonhole stitch, then with the inverse stitch.

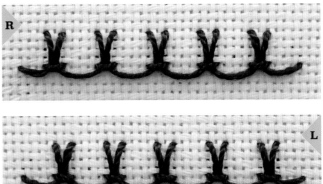

Chevron Stitch

The chevron stitch is another foundation crazy quilting stitch. You can use this versatile stitch in many interesting ways.

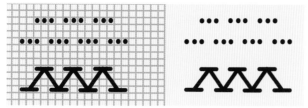

The dot pattern for the basic chevron stitch using seven-count plastic canvas as a guide. (Refer to Marking Your Fabric, page 68.)

1. Bring the thread up from the back of the fabric on the top imaginary line.

2. On the same line, take a stitch so that the needle emerges in the middle. Pull the needle through with the thread below the stitch.

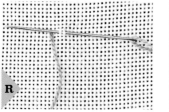

3. Take the needle diagonally and insert it on the bottom line. Bring the needle back up along the same line.

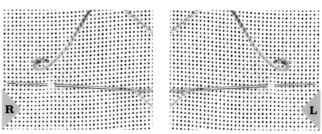

4. Pull the needle through. On the same line, insert the needle so that it emerges in the middle. Pull the needle through to make the foot of the stitch, bringing it up at the base of the diagonal stitch.

5. Take your needle to the top line and repeat the process again.

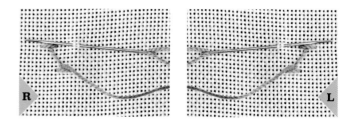

6. Repeat this process, alternating up and down.

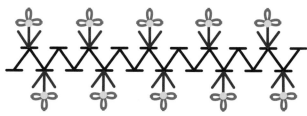

Work small motifs on the feet of a chevron stitch. Three detached chain stitches and some straight stitches make a simple decoration. You can complete these with a French knot in the middle or add seed beads for extra zing.

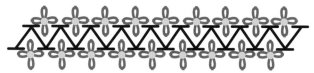

There are numerous ways of using the triangular spaces created by a line of chevron stitches. Add decorative motifs in the triangular spaces. On the second pass, add four detached chain stitches and a French knot or seed bead to make a lovely band.

Space decorative motifs at intervals along the line. Quarter-buttonhole rings are tucked into the triangular spaces. Add a seed bead or French knot.

Widen the line by adding to the height of the chevron stitch. Add half-buttonhole rings and a seed bead to emphasize the zigzag movement of the chevron stitch. Repeated elements like this always create an interesting seam decoration.

Extend the height of the motifs. Create a change of scale by working three-quarter buttonhole rings on top of a straight-stitch stem. Finish with seed beads or French knots.

This pattern extends the height of the motifs and echoes the zigzag of the chevron stitch using the design principles of scale and repetition to create movement.

For a totally different look, overlap the stitch and change the density, so it becomes a double chevron stitch. Use two different-colored threads to add even more interest.

tip A line of double chevron stitches is also ideal for couching a ribbon along a seam. Baste the ribbon in place, and then work two rows of chevron stitches over the ribbon.

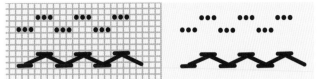

This dot pattern changes the height of the chevron stitch and creates different-sized triangular spaces, allowing you even more options. The line of stitching created means that any decoration you use is spaced further apart and will give the line of stitching a lighter feel.

Decorate the line with motifs, such as a circle of seed beads or French knots sitting on top of a straight-stitch stem and two detached chain stitches for leaves.

If the line is looking a bit predictable, change the angle of your stitches to create more movement.

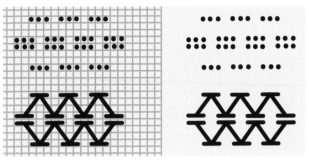

This dot pattern is two rows of chevron stitches back to back.

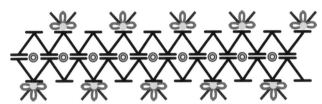

Working two rows back to back creates many more spaces to tuck beads or small motifs into. The second pass of stitches can be worked above or between each horizontal bar. You can also add beads and sequins.

Work two foundation lines of chevron stitches slightly apart to create a space for adding stitches down the middle.

When you need an even wider line of embroidery over a seam, add motifs along the outside edge in the triangular spaces.

Offset each row to create a different pattern with small spaces that are ideal for beads or small motifs.

Add a third row of stitching to create a different space to work a small motif or add a bead or sequin.

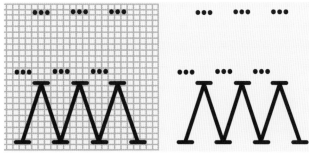

This dot pattern forms a very wide chevron stitch. Contrast the size and scale of your stitches. Use a thread that is a slightly heavier weight, such as cotton perle #5. A thin thread used on a wide pattern can look sparse. Don't be afraid to be dramatic.

A wide zigzag creates enough space for a second motif to be easily worked over the chevron stitch.

Since the spacing is wider and further apart, you can also tuck motifs in between the horizontal bars of the stitch.

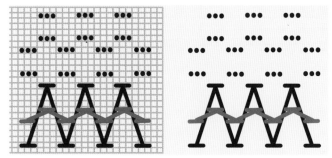

This dot pattern increases the height of the stitch to give more room for a second foundation row of chevron stitches worked over the top of the first.

The second row of chevron stitches creates a pattern of spaces that are ideal for further decoration, either inside or outside the line of the stitches. An alternative is to work the second row using a beaded chevron stitch.

Motifs placed just outside the main row will expand the line, which will strengthen the seam area visually. Use this stronger line when you need to balance another element on your block.

You have wiggle room to use a slightly larger motif because of the tall foundation row. A half–buttonhole wheel and straight stitches create little flower motifs.

Play with the spacing of stitches and change the density, working closely together or further apart. Have fun. Add beads, overlap the stitch, or use it to couch down another thread or ribbon.

BEADED CHEVRON STITCH

Use a tapestry #26 needle to bead stitches as you work. A seven-count plastic canvas can act as guide to mark one of the chevron dot patterns (pages 84, 86, and 87).

1. Bring the thread up from the back of the fabric on the top imaginary line. Thread 2 or 3 seed beads onto your working thread.

2. On the same line, insert the needle and bring it up in the middle. Pull the needle through to make a small stitch, with the needle below the stitch.

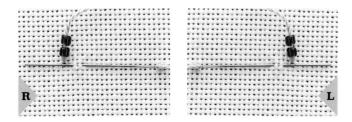

3. Take the needle diagonally and insert it on the bottom line. Bring it back up along the same line.

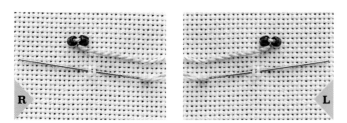

4. Pull the needle through. Thread 2 or 3 seed beads onto your thread. On the same line, insert the needle and bring it back up in the middle. Pull the needle through to make

the foot of the stitch by having it emerge at the base of the diagonal stitch.

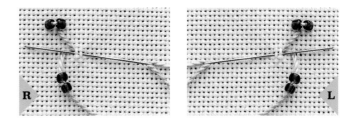

5. Take your needle to the top line and repeat the process again.

6. Repeat this process, alternating up and down.

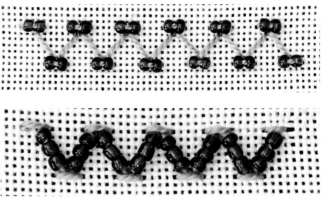

As an alternative, add beads to the diagonal stitches.

tip To gauge the number of beads you need on your thread, lay a few beads against the stitch and see what number will fit. When you change the scale of your stitch, you will need to adjust the number of beads accordingly.

:: Beaded chevron worked over rickrack

:: You can also substitute seed beads for bugle beads or any bead that will fit.

:: It is fun to work a line of regular chevron stitches and then space a second beaded row of chevron stitches
:: in between the first row.

Cretan Stitch

Once you get in the rhythm, the Cretan stitch is a quick and easy stitch to work and offers you many opportunities for decorating your crazy quilt projects.

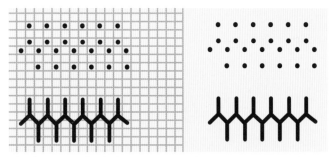

The dot pattern for the basic Cretan stitch, using seven-count plastic canvas as a guide. (Refer to Marking Your Fabric, page 68.)

1. Bring the needle up from the back of the fabric at the start of the line. Insert the needle on the top edge to make a small stitch by pointing the needle to the center.

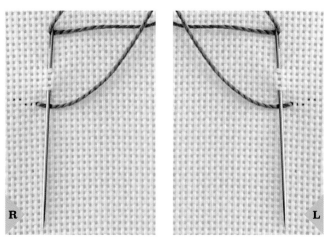

2. Keep the thread under the needle and pull it through the fabric.

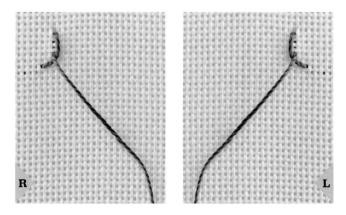

3. Move to the lower edge of the row and repeat.

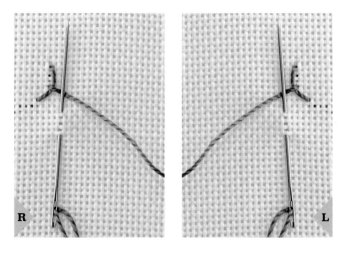

4. Make sure that with each small stitch the needle points to the middle of the line and the thread is caught under the needle before you pull it through.

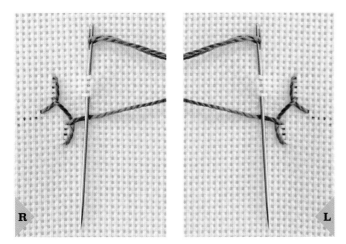

5. Continue working along the line.

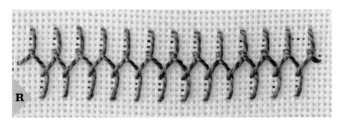

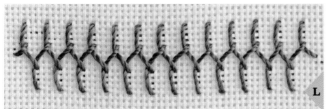

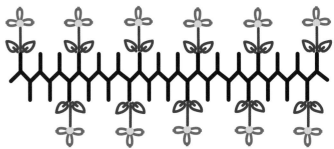

Use three detached chain stitches and some straight stitches as a simple flower design.

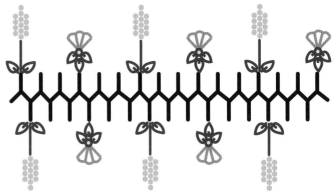

Widen the line by adding to the height of the elements. These floral motifs can be created using French knots and a quarter-buttonhole ring. The leaves are detached chain stitches. A wide seam decoration such as this will make the seam and that area of a block visually stronger. You can use this stronger line to balance another element on your block.

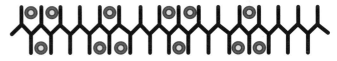

Place decorative motifs in the spaces created between the arms of the stitch to create a secondary pattern with small motifs, beads, or sequins.

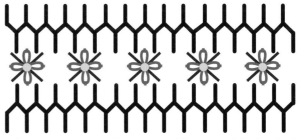

A fun variation is to work two rows of Cretan stitch back to back and use the space between them to create a decorative centerline.

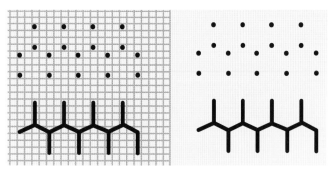

Use this dot pattern to vary the spacing of the arms of the Cretan stitch.

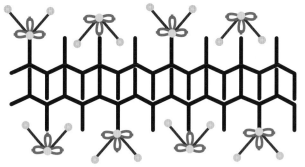

Work with two lines of Cretan stitch, offset and slightly overlapping. It creates a totally different look and opens up different opportunities to create decorative patterns.

The larger area between the stitches allows you to add motifs at a different angle. The contrast in angle creates movement and variety, so the seam decoration looks different. Changing the angle of the stitches can add interest.

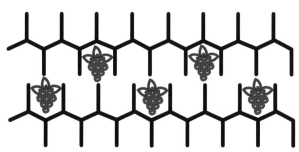

Two rows are offset and slightly pulled apart, providing space to fit slightly larger motifs, such as bunches of grapes created from French knots and detached chain stitches.

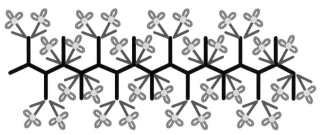

Add more movement to the seam by extending the height of the angled motifs. Adding height also makes a wider seam, which creates a stronger visual impact.

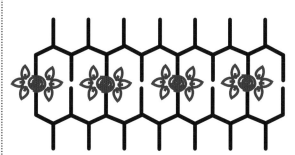

Work two lines of Cretan stitch face to face and place a small motif between them, which creates a secondary line. Add bullion roses and leaves worked in a detached chain stitch.

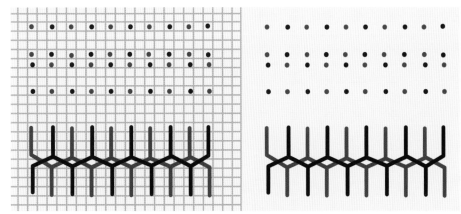

The dot pattern for overlapping two lines of Cretan stitches provides more opportunities to decorate your crazy quilt seams. Work a line of Cretan stitches in two passes. Each pass in the diagram is marked with a different color so you can see the first and second passes.

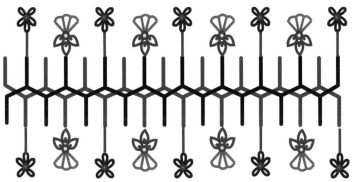

Add embroidery to the top and bottom arms of the stitch. This makes a wide dramatic seam to help manage the composition of your block.

Add embroidery or beading to the spaces in between the arms of the stitch. This secondary pattern can be used to your advantage because the complexity of patterns attracts the eye and creates interest.

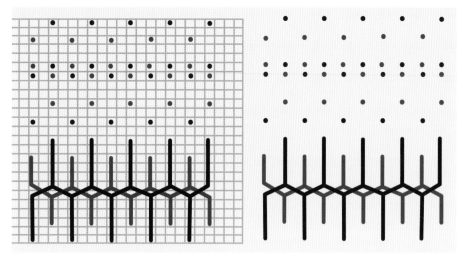

Use this dot pattern to change the arm height of the Cretan stitch. This grid pattern is marked with two colors in order to clearly differentiate the two overlapping foundation lines of stitching.

Decorate each side of the line.

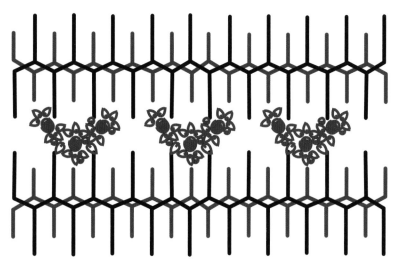

Work two lines slightly apart to allow space for a secondary motif—in this case, a small garland of bullion roses with detached chain-stitch foliage.

BEADED CRETAN STITCH

Using the beaded version of the Cretan stitch can take your crazy quilt projects to another level. You can bead the central spine or the arms of the Cretan stitch, or you can create a pattern by beading every second arm or every fifth arm or whatever pattern you choose. This beaded version of the Cretan stitch can be worked using the grids shown in Cretan stitch (pages 90 and 92–94). As with all the beaded stitches, use a tapestry #26 needle.

1. Bring the needle up through the fabric at the start of the line. Thread 2 or 3 seed beads onto your working thread.

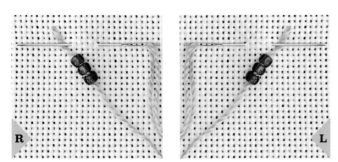

2. Keep the thread under the needle and pull it through the fabric. Insert the needle on the outside edge. Make a small stitch by pointing the needle to the center and keeping the thread under the needle as you pull it through your fabric. As you pull the thread through, nudge your beads into place on the arm of the first stitch.

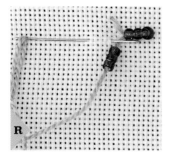 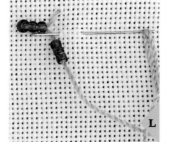

3. Continue down the line, adding beads to one side and then the other. The trick is to remember that the needle points towards the middle and catches the thread under the needle with each stitch.

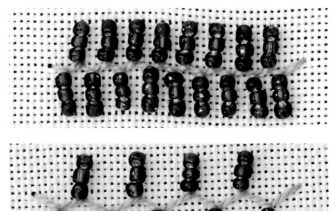

Change the spacing of the Cretan stitch to create different patterns.

tip Change the height of the arms, or bead every second arm along the line. You can also add beads down the central spine by threading one bead on the working thread and nudging it to center of the line of the stitch rather than outward on the arm of the stitch. Experiment and have fun!

Feather stitch

The feather stitch is one of the most popular foundation stitches because of its versatility. You can work it along a seam or let it meander across a block. Its organic feel is ideal for floral sprays; you can add many additional decorative stitches to the spines, or tuck beads and stitches in the fork of the spines. Not only is it pretty but also quick to work!

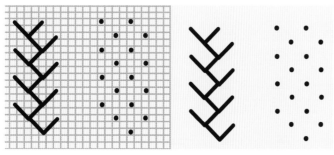

The dot pattern for the basic feather stitch using seven-count plastic canvas as a guide (refer to Marking Your Fabric, page 68). Once you master the stitch, you can work it in a free-form, organic manner.

1. Bring the thread up from the back of the fabric at the top of where you want to create the stitch. Insert the needle next to and even with the point where the thread emerged, and come up below and between the 2 points, looping the working thread under the needle.

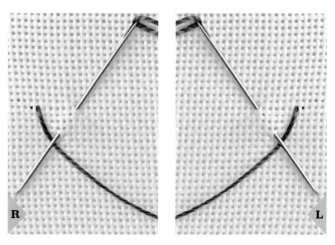

2. Pull the thread; it should make a V. Insert the needle on the other side, next to and even with the point where the thread emerged, and come up below and between the 2 points, looping the working thread under the needle.

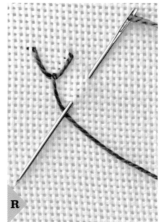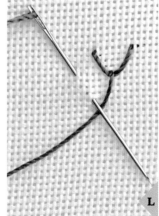

3. Repeat this process.

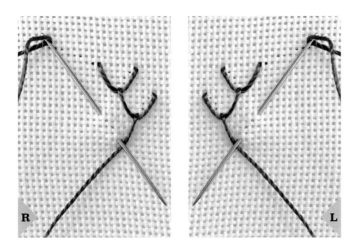

4. Work these stitches, alternating from side to side.

Add small floral motifs or beads to the fork of each stitch. I have illustrated detached chain stitches and French knots, but as with all these patterns, you can use any of the motif stitches (page 118) with sequins or beads.

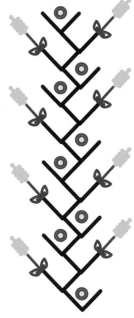

Creating a secondary pattern along the stitch is easy. Establish a line of motifs or beads tucked in the forks, and then add a second pattern to the arms. Combine small motifs, such as a grouping of French knots and detached chain leaves spaced along every second arm of the feather-stitch line.

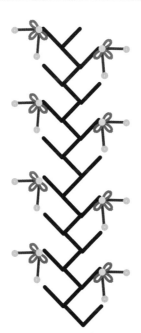

Add decorative motifs to the tip of each arm.

Stitch a sequin or bead to the base of each fork to create another type of pattern.

:: Bugle beads tucked into the fork of a feather stitch

:: Feather stitch decorated with metal novelty beads and bugle beads

:: Beaded feather stitch

:: Bullion knots tucked into the fork of a feather stitch

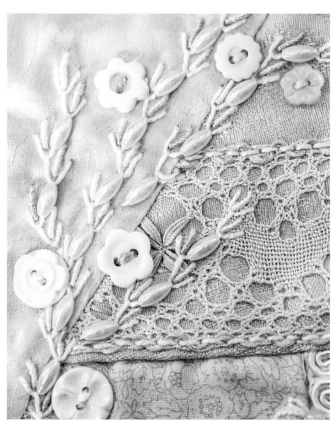

:: The beaded feather stitch lends itself to incorporating larger beads
:: and bugle beads.

BEADED FEATHER STITCH

The feather stitch is tremendously versatile, but you can add even more zest to your crazy quilting by using a beaded feather stitch. You have the option of beading every arm, every second arm, one side of the stitch, or establishing patterns varying which part of the stitch you bead. The variations are all fun to explore.

The number of seed beads you need will be determined by the size of your stitch. Lay 3 or 4 beads against your stitching to work out the number you require. Use a tapestry #26 needle and the grid dot pattern for feather stitch (page 96).

1. Bring the thread up from the back of the fabric at the top of where you want to create the stitch. Thread 3 seed beads onto your working thread. Insert the needle next to and even with the point where the thread emerged and come up below and between the 2 points, looping the working thread under the needle.

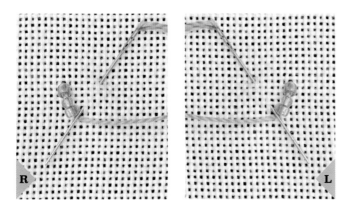

2. Pull the thread, adjusting the beads into position; it should make a V. Thread 3 seed beads onto your working thread. Insert the needle on the other side, next to and even with the point where the thread emerged, and come up below and between the 2 points, looping the working thread under the needle.

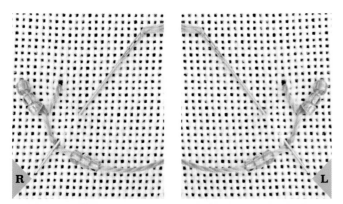

3. Repeat this process.

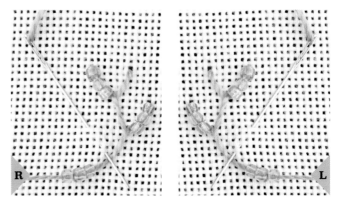

4. Work these stitches, alternating from side to side.

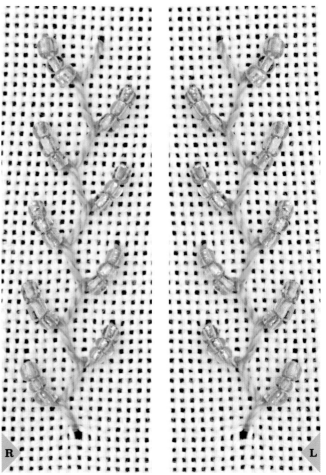

UP AND DOWN FEATHER STITCH

The up and down feather stitch is worked in a manner similar to the feather stitch. It produces an interesting feathery line of twin stitches tied with a bar. It can be used for organic twiggy bits in floral motifs because it follows a curve well. It can also be the foundation for a seam embellishment stitch.

The instructions may look complex, but once you are familiar with it, the stitch has a pleasant rhythm. Before learning this stitch, be familiar with both the feather stitch and the up and down buttonhole stitch.

1. Bring the thread up from the back of the fabric at the top of where you want to create the stitch. Insert the needle next to and even with the point where the thread emerged, and come up below and between the 2 points, looping the working thread under the needle.

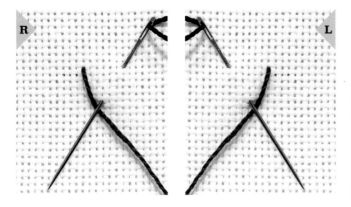

2. For the second stitch of the pair, when you bring the needle up through the fabric, point the needle in the opposite direction. In other words, point the needle outward.

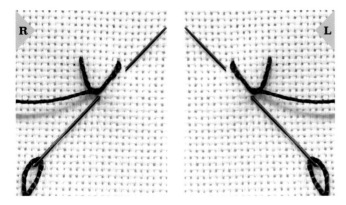

3. Wrap the thread under the needle at the top.

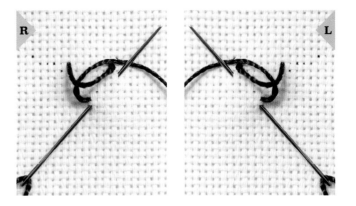

4. Pull the needle through the fabric. As you do this, pull the thread in and toward you to catch the loop that forms. Hold the loop flat against the fabric with your thumb to prevent it from slipping. This loop forms the bar at the base of both stitches. This forms the first pair of tied stitches.

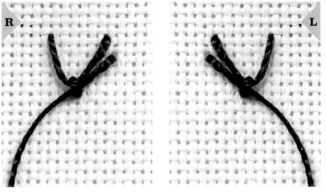

5. Insert the needle on the other side, next to and even with the point where the thread emerged, and come up below and between the 2 points, looping the working thread under the needle.

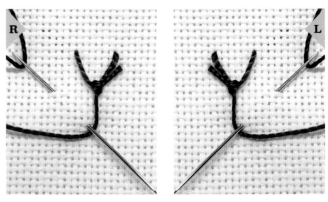

6. Pull the thread taut. Make the second stitch of the pair with the needle pointed outward, and loop the thread under the needle.

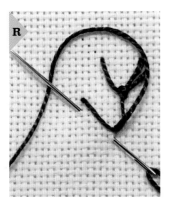 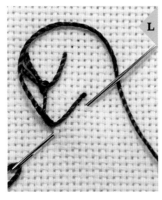

7. Pull the thread through, catching the loop, and hold it flat against the fabric with your other thumb.

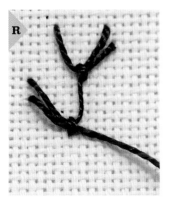 

8. Work these stitches, alternating from side to side.

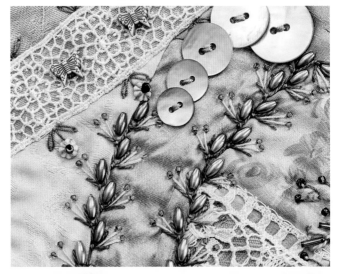

Like the feather stitch, you can change the length and angle of the arms and easily add motifs and beads.

Herringbone Stitch

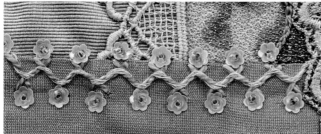

:: Herringbone stitch laced with contrasting thread

Herringbone is another versatile and much-loved stitch used by crazy quilters. It is a highly decorative stitch, particularly if you experiment with the spacing.

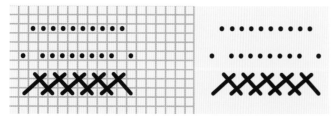

The dot pattern for basic herringbone stitch, using seven-count plastic canvas as a guide. The herringbone stitch is worked along two imaginary horizontal lines.

1. Bring the thread up from the back of the fabric on the lower imaginary line. Make a small stitch on the top line.

2. Pull the thread through. Take the needle diagonally and insert it on the lower line; make a small stitch.

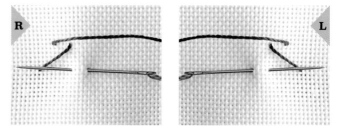

3. Pull the thread through. Take the needle diagonally and insert it on the top line; make a small stitch.

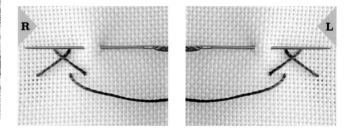

4. Repeat this process along the line.

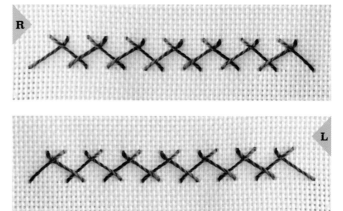

Decorate using a combination of motif stitches (page 118): little floral motifs of French knots and detached chain stitch leaves.

Create a wider decorative seam by using slightly taller motifs. The flowers are created with motif stitches such as detached chain stitches, French knots, and quarter–buttonhole wheels. When mixing motifs, make sure the seam you are decorating is long enough to repeat each motif along the seam at least twice. If there is no repeat, there is no pattern, and it will not have the same effect. Patterns and repeats help tie a block together.

Decorate two foundation rows of herringbone back to back with small motifs—in this case, three detached chain stitches with a seed bead or French knot at the base.

Work two foundation rows slightly apart to add space for a secondary line of stitches.

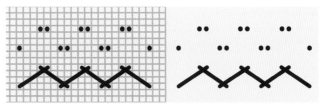

This dot pattern has been stretched to create more space to add decorative elements from the motif stitches (page 118).

Extra space allows you to mix motifs. The space allows you to create a decorative line of hand embroidery that has a light and airy feel.

Add triangle motifs to fit the shape of the spaces.

Decorate the edges of two foundation rows of the herringbone stitch with a line of small motifs. Since the foundation row is stretched to provide more space, the seam decoration has a light and lacy feeling. This pattern would complement a block with a lot of lace or perhaps a spring theme.

Add more space for more ornate motifs and decorations by working two lines of herringbone stitches further apart. There is sufficient space for small floral sprays such as bullion rose garlands. You could also utilize this space by adding some silk ribbon embroidery, larger beads, charms, or a line of buttons.

Four lines of herringbone stitch fill a space and look like a trellis. Bunches of grapes can be created using French knots or beads with small detached chain stitches for leaves.

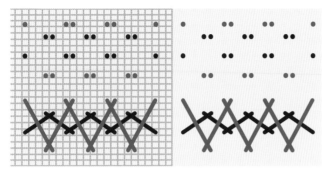

The dot pattern to create two rows of differently spaced and sized herringbone stitches worked on top of each other

Build a wider design by adding motifs to the larger line of herringbone stitches.

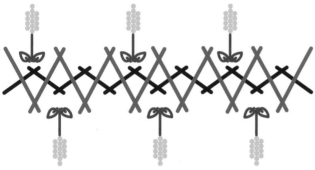

Place a motif above every second cross of the smaller line of herringbone stitches or over every cross. Or create another pattern by placing a motif over every third cross.

Work four foundation lines to produce a complex pattern along a seam. A visually rich seam such as this can balance your composition.

Add beads, sequins, and small motifs, setting up a secondary pattern in the spaces.

Working two separated lines of double herringbone stitches allows for embroidered motifs to be worked between them.

BEADED HERRINGBONE

Beaded herringbone is another variety that makes an ideal stitch to use in crazy quilting. You can use it in conjunction with the dot patterns I have suggested for the herringbone stitch (pages 102–104) or you can develop your own patterns.

tip You can also use beaded herringbone stitches over a satin ribbon. Dealing with a satin ribbon and beads on a slippery fabric is not an easy task, but it is easier if you secure the ribbon with small slip stitches. They do not have to be too perfect, because most of them will be covered with beading, and the beads are what people will notice. Just try to keep the stitches small, so the ribbon is secured and the stitches are not too noticeable.

1. Bring the thread up from the back of the fabric on the bottom left-hand side of the line. Take the needle diagonally and make a small stitch on the top line.

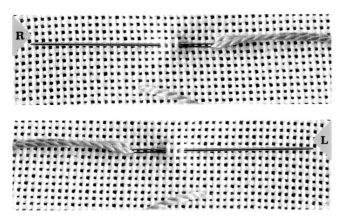

2. Pull the thread through.

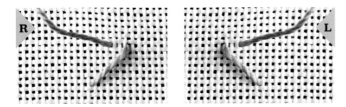

3. Measure your seed beads against the stitch you just made to decide how many you need. Add the required number of seed beads to your thread.

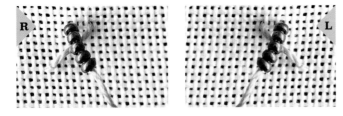

4. Take the needle diagonally and insert on the lower line; make a small stitch.

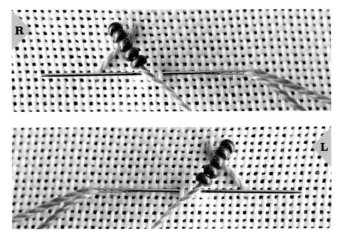

5. Pull the thread through. Take the needle diagonally and insert on the top line; make a small stitch. Pull the thread through.

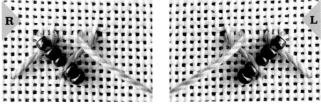

6. Add seed beads to your thread and repeat this process along the line.

LACED HERRINGBONE

One way to enhance an embroidery stitch quickly and easily is to lace it with a contrasting thread or ribbon. Choose many of the wonderful novelty threads and yarns, a metallic thread, or even a fine ribbon. The possibilities are endless. The herringbone stitch is easily and quickly laced. The technique is the same as for lacing the chevron stitch (page 84) or the Cretan stitch (page 90). Laced herringbone stitches can be used with the dot patterns for the herringbone stitch (pages 102–104). Two lines of laced herringbone worked face to face are a very effective seam decoration.

:: Two lines of laced herringbone stitches placed face to face

tip Use a tapestry needle to avoid splitting the foundation stitches, and be careful not to pick up any of the fabric.

1. Work a row of herringbone stitches (pages 102) loosely, because the lacing will tighten the stitches slightly.

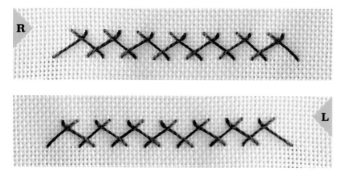

2. Bring the thread up from the back of the fabric on the lower line at the base of the first stitch. Pass the needle under the herringbone crossbar in an upward direction.

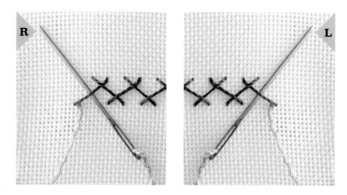

3. Move across the crossbar, turn the needle, and pass it under next bar in a downward direction.

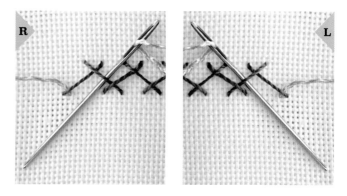

4. Move across the crossbar, turn the needle, and pass it under the next bar in an upward direction.

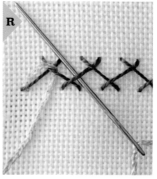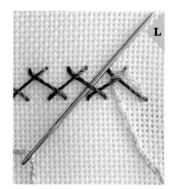

5. Work along the herringbone stitches, keeping the lacing thread slightly loose to avoid distorting the fabric.

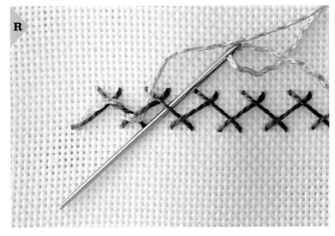

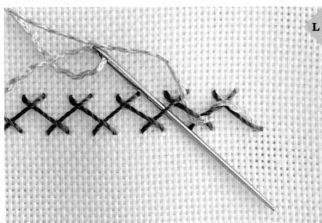

6. Continue lacing until you reach the end of the line

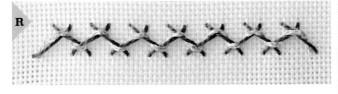

TIED HERRINGBONE

The tied herringbone is another versatile stitch that is quick and easy to work, yet it adds something extra to a line of plain herringbone stitches. You can tie a herringbone stitch in a variety of ways. Choose the one that suits your project.

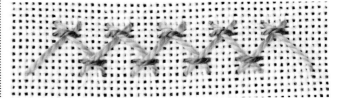

Herringbone stitch tied where the bars cross, usually using a straight stitch. Use any of the dot patterns for herringbone stitch and further enhance them by adding a few stitches.

Herringbone stitch tied with an upright cross-stitch. Herringbone stitches can be tied with a French knot, various cross-stitches, bullion knots, sequins, seed beads, or bugle beads.

Herringbone stitch tied with a detached chain stitch

Herringbone stitch tied with a straight stitch and decorated with small motifs and beads

Linear Stitches for Motifs and Flourishes

Linear stitches are usually used to embroider anything that is defined by a line, such as the outside line of fans, horseshoes, bows, and the like. Linear stitches are also useful for stems of flowers, vines, or tendrils. Monograms, letters, and dates are also situations where you would choose a linear stitch. If your quilt has a theme, you might want to stitch the outline of a motif that relates to the theme, like the outline of teacup on a patch in your crazy quilt project with a teatime theme.

Individual small designs are often embroidered using linear stitches. These hearts would be ideal to work in backstitches or chain stitches.

A few lines of stem stitches added to a group of three fargo roses to tie them together

Heart shapes are defined with stem stitches, which are one of the most popular linear stitches.

tip Three tips for choosing hand embroidery patterns:

- Keep it small and simple. Find a motif small enough to fit the patch on your block and simple enough to be embellished further. Look for motifs with a simple outline that have natural opportunities to add beads.

- If you can't keep it simple, make it a point of emphasis. If a design has a real wow factor, make it a point of emphasis.

- Adapt and design your own. Start with simple patterns and shapes such as hearts, paisley shapes, teacups, horseshoes, butterflies, or small floral sprays. At first, adapt and change commercial patterns to fit your needs, and before long you will be designing your own.

Linear stitches include the backstitch, stem stitch, and chain stitch, and can often be used interchangeably. These stitches can all be whipped (see Whipped Backstitch, page 111) to make a firmer stitch and in some cases, a neater line. Some of these stitches produce a finer line than others. Often, personal taste rather than technical reasons dictates the choice.

A linear stitch can tie a line of small designs together. This is an example of chain stitches that have been whipped.

A pattern such as this can be worked mainly in stem stitches, with the flower petals being detached chain stitches.

A second floral pattern can be worked using the stem stitch. The middle of the flowers could be French knots or beads.

You can also use linear stitches to create seam embellishments. This type of design is usually created using a template. For information on marking your lines and using templates, see Using Templates as a Guide for Stitches (page 70). You can also trace around items such as coins or make your own templates from quilter's plastic.

Treat a linear stitch like a foundation stitch. Patterns that have sharp points like this one are best worked in a backstitch or running stitch.

Work two sets back to back.

Many of the linear patterns created using templates are easily over-lapped to create different patterns.

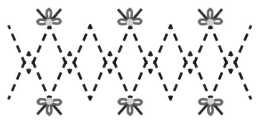

This linear pattern is created by tracing a template and adding a second overlapping line before adding motif stitches.

Work two lines side by side for greater effect.

Work two double lines overlapped. The backstitch, whipped backstitch, stem stitch, or chain stitch can be used to embroider this pattern.

Double lines can be pulled apart and a secondary pattern can be created with small motifs.

Use a template to create curves. Here, the line weaves in and out of a line of flowers created by using detached chain stitches.

Stitch scallops; then add motifs on the second pass. The stem stitch is ideal for making scallops.

Two lines of scallops face to face provide space along the middle line in which to work other small motifs.

Backstitch

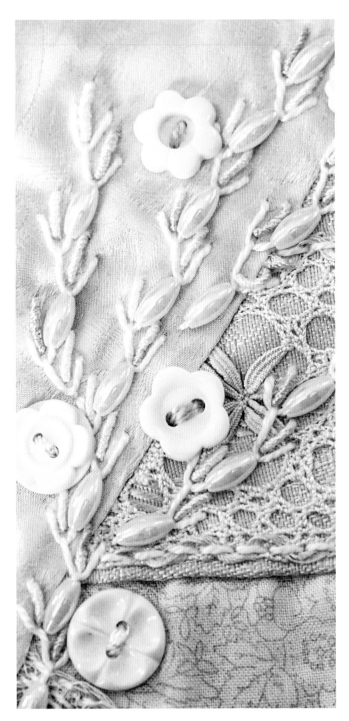

The backstitch is a useful linear stitch that can be easily whipped (see Whipped Backstitch, next page).

1. Bring the thread up from the back of the fabric on the imaginary line. Make a small backward stitch. Take a bite of the fabric, and have the needle emerge a little in front of the first stitch but still on the same imaginary line. Pull the thread through the fabric.

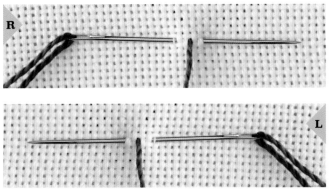

2. Make the second stitch backward, inserting the needle down into the hole made by the first stitch and bringing the needle out a little in front of the second stitch but still on the line.

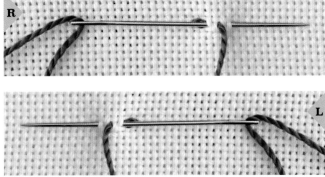

3. Repeat this process along the line.

WHIPPED BACKSTITCH

:: Whipped backstitch scallops

A whipped backstitch creates a slightly raised line that is simple, quick, and easy to work. The chain stitch, stem stitch, and running stitch can all be whipped using the same technique. Each produces a slightly different-looking line. Some are more raised than others, and some follow a curve with more ease, so experiment in order to get the look you want.

If you whip with a heavy thread in the same color as the foundation stitching, the line you sew will look like a fine cord. This technique is also useful if you want a raised line on a delicate, fine fabric that can't accept a heavy thread through the weave. This stitch can also be worked with variations of contrasting color, producing a candy cane effect or a lightly textured thread.

tip Use a blunt-ended tapestry needle for the second thread, so you do not split the foundation threads as you sew.

1. Work a foundation row of backstitches (previous page). Make each stitch slightly longer and looser than usual. To whip the row, bring the needle up from the back of the fabric and pass the needle under the first stitch.

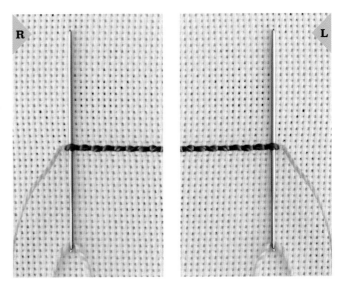

2. Take the thread over the top and slide the needle under the second backstitch. Do not pick up any of the fabric, as it is a lacing action, not a stitching movement.

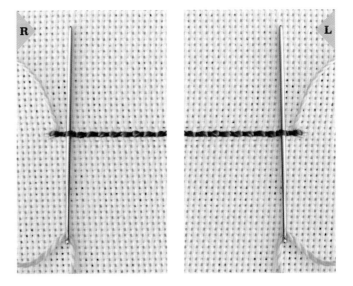

3. Repeat this until you have whipped the length of the row.

Chain Stitch

::: Chain-stitched scallops that are then embroidered with fargo roses, leaf stitches, straight stitches, and beads

::: The chain stitch can also be used in a more delicate manner. This V-shaped line of stitches runs alongside a bugle bead that is about ¼″ (0.6 cm) long.

::: The chain stitch is a good choice if you want to follow a curve.

::: The chain stitch looks good in thread that has a firm twist, such as perle cotton #8. In this sample, each chain is about the size of a seed bead.

The chain stitch is tremendously versatile stitch, because it follows a curve so well yet can also define a straight line. It is slightly wider than a stem stitch or a backstitch. So if you want a line that is a little thicker than a stem stitch, the chain stitch is a good choice.

To make a whipped chain stitch, see Whipped Backstitch (page 111).

1. Bring the needle up from the back of the fabric. Insert the needle back into where it emerged. Bring the point of the needle out a short space along the line to be stitched.

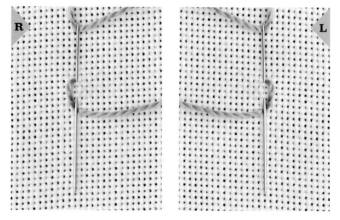

2. With the thread wrapped under the needle, pull the needle through the fabric to make the first stitch.

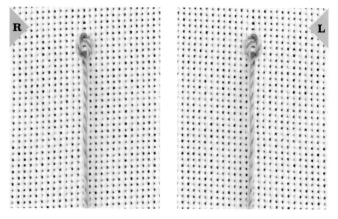

3. Insert the needle into the middle of the chain stitch where it emerged, bringing the point out further along the line. Once again, wrap the thread under the needle and pull through.

4. Continue in this manner along the line.

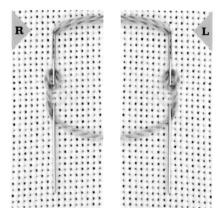

ZIGZAG CHAIN STITCH

:: Zigzag chain stitch worked over rickrack

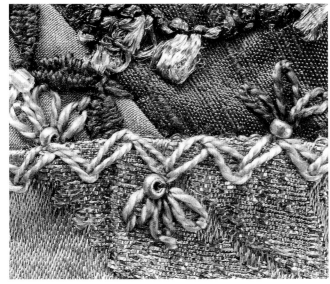

:: Zigzag chain stitch worked as a foundation stitch on a seam

The zigzag chain stitch is a fun variation of the chain stitch.

1. Bring the needle up from the back on the top imaginary line, and insert the needle back into the same hole where it came out. Take a bite of the fabric to have the needle emerge on the bottom line a short diagonal space along. With the thread under the needle, pull the needle through the fabric.

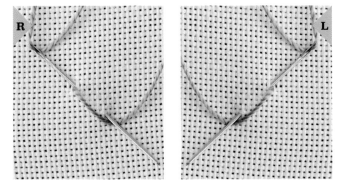

2. Insert your needle back where it came up through the fabric, and take a bite of the fabric to have the needle emerge on the top line a short diagonal space along. With the thread wrapped under the needle, pull the needle through the fabric.

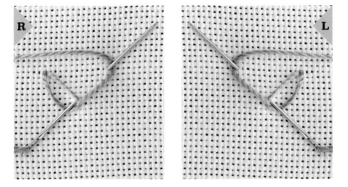

3. Continue along the line, working each loop at a right angle to the previous loop to create the zigzag line.

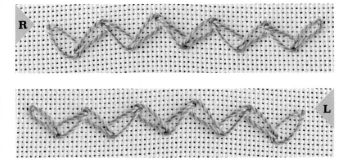

If your loops flip up, the solution is to catch the loop with your needle as it enters the fabric. Pierce the end of the previous loop to ensure that each section of the chain lies flat.

Couching

:: Couched threads form the stems of these novelty bead flowers.

:: A synthetic knitting ribbon twisted together with metallic thread was couched to the block before adding the French knot grapes.

:: A couched textured novelty yarn

Couching is not a stitch but a technique that will easily create a line. A surface thread is laid on the fabric and then anchored using a second thread. The stitches used to secure the thread can be small overcast stitches or decorative embroidery stitches. Stitches such as the herringbone, Cretan, buttonhole, and chevron stitch, just to name just a few, can be used to couch braids, ribbon, and lace.

Couching is ideal for stems, vines, and tendrils. Lay down a thick thread, establish the main lines of a design, and then get on with the fun bits of the motif.

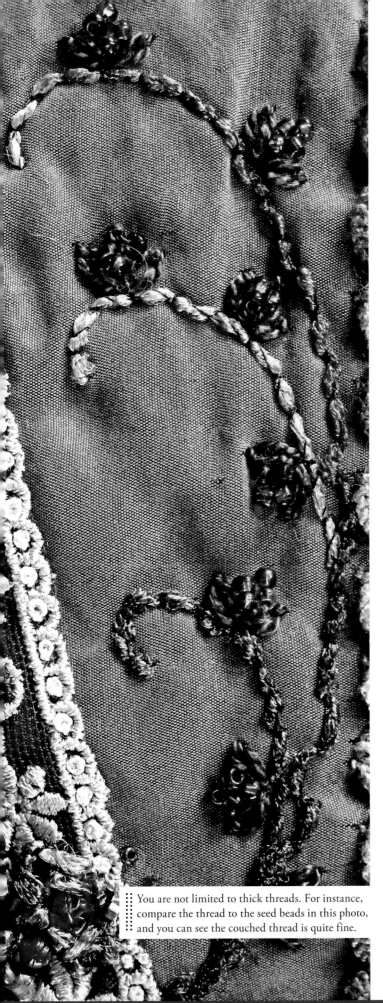

Any kind of thread can be couched to fabric. Thick wool, novelty yarns, and light cords can all be used to great effect. All those hairy, fluffy, bobbly, shiny, metallic fibers you find can be used.

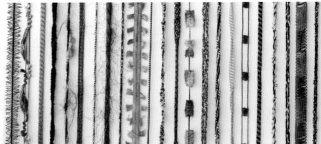

⋮⋮ Some of the novelty yarns that can be couched onto fabric.

--------------------------------- NOTE ---------------------------------

In this sample, I used a contrasting colored thread to secure the thicker thread and to make the couching stitch more visible. Normally you would match the color of the working thread to the thread you are couching.

1. Using a large-eyed needle, bring the heavy thread up from the back of the fabric. Using a finer needle and thread, make small, straight stitches over the thick thread to secure it to the fabric until you have completed the line.

2. Take the end of heavy thread to the back of the fabric using a large-eyed needle. Secure both ends with small stitches using the fine thread. Do not clip the heavy thread too close, or it will pop up to the surface.

tip The couched thread can also be split, knotted, looped, plaited, or teased out into tufts. Two threads can be twisted together, beads can be added to the couching thread—anything you can think of. Couching is an effective way to add interest to any crazy quilt project.

⋮⋮ You are not limited to thick threads. For instance, compare the thread to the seed beads in this photo, and you can see the couched thread is quite fine.

Running Stitch

Many people know the running stitch as a quilting stitch, but in surface embroidery it is often used as a linear stitch.

To work this stitch, simply pass the needle over and under the fabric in a regular, even manner

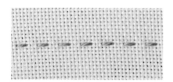

To make a whipped running stitch, see Whipped Backstitch (page 111).

THREADED RUNNING STITCH

In surface embroidery, 2 lines of running stitches can be the foundation of many interesting lacing patterns. This can be used as a seam decoration or as a thicker linear stitch. Lines of running stitches can be laced with novelty threads or a fine ribbon.

Use a tapestry needle to avoid splitting the foundation stitches, and take care to lace and not to pick up any of the fabric.

1. Work 2 lines of running stitches, with the second line offset from the first. Make each stitch slightly loose but not floppy. As you weave the lacing in and out, the foundation stitches will tighten slightly.

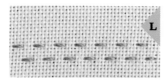

2. Bring the thread up from the back on the outside of the first stitch on the lower line. Pass the needle under the first stitch, then under the first stitch on the top line, threading in an upward direction. Pull the lacing thread through.

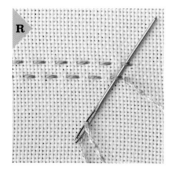
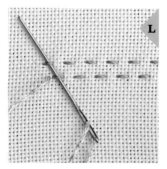

3. Pass your needle under the second running stitch on the top row, angle the needle downward, and pass it under the first stitch on the bottom line. Pull the lacing thread through.

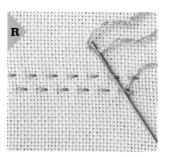
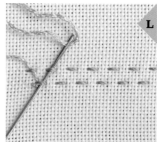

4. Move along the bottom line and pass the needle under the second stitch on the bottom line and angle the needle to pass it under the second stitch on the top line.

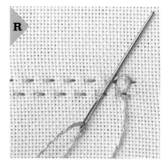
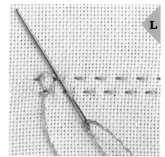

5. Work along the line, moving from top to bottom, alternating the lacing. Keeping the lacing thread slightly loose to avoid distorting the fabric.

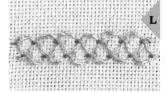

6. When you reach the end, take the lacing thread to the back of the fabric and tie off.

Stem Stitch

:: Use the stem stitch in a tight curve.

:: Stem stitches along a crazy quilt seam

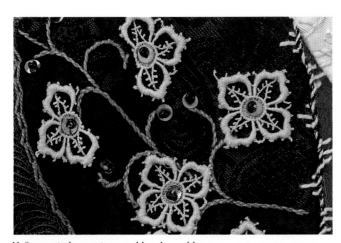

:: Stem stitch, sequins, seed beads, and lace

The stem stitch is one of my go-to stitches to outline shapes, make stems for foliage, and make scallops and curved lines along a seam. You can work the stem stitch with silk ribbon.

To make a whipped stem stitch, see Whipped Backstitch (page 111).

1. Bring the thread up from the back of the fabric. With your working thread under your needle, make a small stitch.

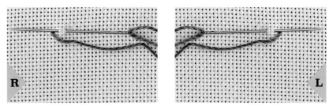

2. Pull the thread through the fabric and make the second stitch, bringing the needle out a little behind the first stitch.

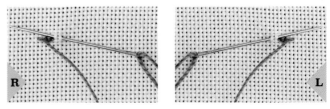

3. Repeat this process along the line. Keep the stitches the same length and the tension even. If your stitch does not look neat, work them closer together. The closer the stitches are spaced, the tighter the line.

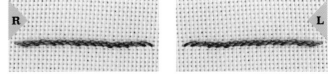

:: The stem stitch is also used in silk ribbon embroidery. The stems for the tulips in this sample were worked in the stem stitch using 4 mm silk ribbon.

Motif Stitches

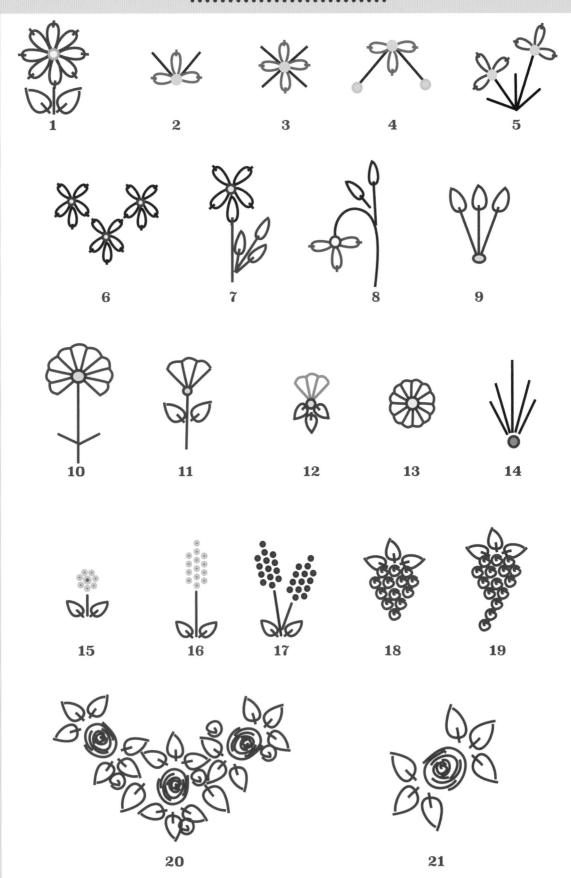

Key to motif stitches

Motif stitches can be used in single or multiple units. They can be thought of as little designs in their own right. A very popular motif is the detached chain stitch (or lazy daisy stitch) arranged in a circle to form a daisy. Motif stitches can be combined with foundation seam stitches to produce an infinite variety of patterns that can be used to decorate crazy quilt seams. There are numerous other stitches that can be used for small motifs, which you can explore once these are mastered.

1. The detached chain-stitch daisy is made of eight detached chain stitches, a stem of straight stitches, and leaves of detached chain stitches, with a French knot or bead in the middle.

2. Detached chain stitches arranged in a half-fan with straight stitches worked in between and a French knot or bead at the base

3. A square of detached chain and straight stitches, with a French knot or bead in the middle

4. A set of three detached chain stitches with extended straight stitches worked in between and a French knot or bead at the head

5. A set of two flowers made of detached chain stitches with straight-stitch stems and a French knot or bead to complete the little flowers

6. Flowers made of five detached chain stitches with a bead or French knot in the middle of each flower

7. A flower of five detached chain stitches with a bead or French knot in the middle. The stem is made of straight stitches and the leaves are detached chain stitches.

8. A flower head of three detached chain stitches with a bead or French knot in the middle. The stem stitch was used for the curve of the stem and the leaves are detached chain stitches on a stem of straight stitches.

9. A small fan of three detached chain stitches with a long tie off or straight stitch

10. A flower made of a buttonhole wheel that is worked three-quarters of the way around with a stem of straight stitches and a French knot or bead in the middle

11. A quarter–buttonhole wheel with a stem of straight stitches, leaves of detached chain stitches, and a French knot or bead at the base of the flower

12. A quarter–buttonhole wheel with detached chain leaves at the base and a French knot or bead at the middle of the flower

13. A buttonhole wheel flower with a French knot or bead in the middle

14. Straight stitches arranged in a fan with a French knot or bead at the base

15. Small circle of French knots or beads with a straight-stitch stem and detached chain leaves

16. A tall flower made of French knots or beads with a straight-stitch stem and detached chain leaves

17. Two tall flowers set at an angle, made of French knots or beads, with a straight-stitch stem and detached chain leaves

18. A cluster of grapes or wisteria made of French knots or beads with detached chain-stitch leaves

19. Grapes or wisteria with a longer drape made of more French knots or beads with detached chain-stitch leaves

20. A small floral garland of bullion roses, woven roses, or fargo roses with detached chain-stitch leaves

21. A bullion rose, woven rose, or fargo rose with detached chain-stitch leaves

Bullion Knot

:: Bullion knots worked between the forks of feather stitches

:: Bullion knots used as flower buds on a crazy quilt

Bullion knots create wonderful organic shapes such as buds or roses. You can easily tuck them along a seam once you have mastered this stitch.

- Stretch the fabric in a needlework hoop or frame, so you have both hands free to work the knot.

- When you are first learning how to stitch a bullion knot, start with a simple four- or five-wrap bullion. Then as you master those, you can add more wraps to your bullions.

1. Bring the thread up from the back of the fabric and take a small stitch, bringing the needle back up near where it first came out of the fabric. The distance between these 2 points determines the length of the knot.

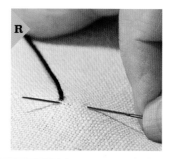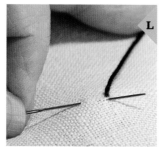

2. Wrap the thread round the needle 5 or 6 times. The wound thread on the needle should be the same length as the small stitch.

3. Gently pull the needle through the coiled thread while holding the coil between your first finger and thumb. This will keep the coil smooth and prevent it from knotting. Pull the working thread up and away from you.

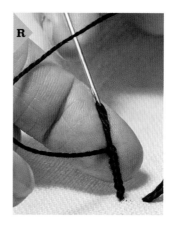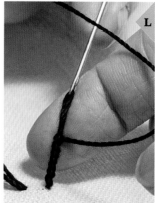

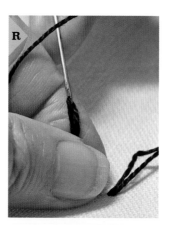

4. As the coil tightens, change the direction you are pulling the thread, and pull it toward you.

5. If the bullion bunches or looks untidy, pass the needle under the bullion and rub it up and down the length of the bullion to smooth out the coils. Stitchers call this *rubbing the belly of the bullion.*

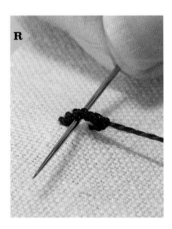
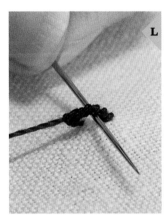

6. When the bullion is smooth, take the needle through the fabric at the point where the thread first emerged.

7. The coil of thread should now lie neatly on the surface.

tips

- If you have trouble with a knot that is too tight or with sliding the knot down the needle, use a milliners or straw needle. Milliners and straw needles have an eye and shaft that are the same diameter, which makes sliding the wrapped bullion knot along the needle easy.

- If stranded cotton threads tangle, try a twisted thread such as perle cotton #5 or #8.

- If your thread tangles and untwists, wrap the bullion in the opposite direction around the needle, so wrap follows the direction in which the thread was spun.

BULLION ROSE

⋮⋮ Bullion roses worked in wool

Bullion roses always charm viewers. They can be used in floral sprays and worked large or small. There are many variations, but all of them involve working the "petals" around in a circle, overlapping the bullions as you go. Start with 2 small bullion stitches, 3 French knots, or a center bead.

1. Work 2 bullion knots (page 120) side by side. Each bullion knot should have 4 to 6 wraps.

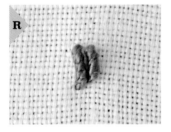 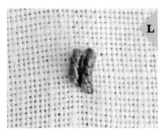

2. For the first petal, make a bullion knot of 9 or 10 wraps at a 45°–50° angle to the first stitch, as shown.

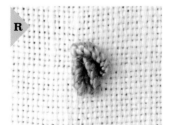 

3. Work the next petal, overlapping the first petal as shown.

4. Continue around in a circle, each time making sure the needle comes out behind the previous bullion.

5. Each bullion stitch overlaps the previous bullion.

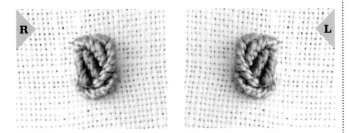

6. Gradually increase the number of wraps and the angle, so each petal is a little longer than the previous one.

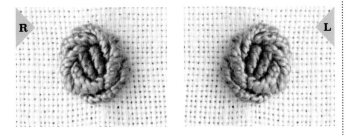

7. To complete your rose, add leaves using the leaf stitch or detached chain stitches and 4 mm silk ribbon.

BULLION BUDS

1. Bullion buds are simply 2 bullion knots worked side by side.

2. Add a fly stitch (page 131) to the base and you have a bud. In this sample I used 4 mm silk ribbon.

Buttonhole Wheel

:: Quarter–buttonhole wheels

:: Buttonhole wheel with a whipped edge (see Whipped Backstitch,
:: page 111).

:: Half–buttonhole wheels worked along a seam with flower-shaped
:: sequins that have been cut in half and stitched down

Buttonhole wheels are wonderfully versatile. Worked whole, they create flowers; worked in halves and quarters, they can be arranged along a line. They are simply a buttonhole stitch worked in a circle.

1. Using a removable pen or pencil, draw a circle with a dot in the middle on your fabric.

2. Bring the thread up from the back of the fabric on the outer edge of the circle. Insert the needle into the center of the circle and come out on the circle a little to the side of the original exit point. Loop the thread under the needle.

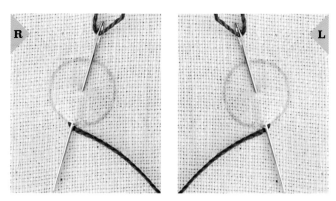

3. Pull the needle through the fabric to form the first spoke of the wheel. Insert the needle into the center again and come out on the circle next to the last spoke, keeping the thread under the needle to make the second spoke.

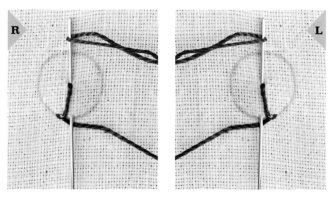

4. Repeat Step 3 to make more spokes.

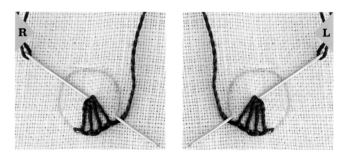

5. Continue stitching spokes to complete the wheel.

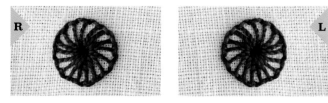

tip If the edge of your wheel flips up, work your stitches closer together.

Detached Chain Stitch

:: Detached chain stitch worked in sets of three along the base of some
:: lace. Straight stitches and seed beads complete the motif.

:: Detached chain stitch used in groups of three to secure some lace

The detached chain stitch, also known as the *lazy daisy stitch*, is a long-time favorite because it can be used to create little flowers and leaves. Its simplicity makes it tremendously versatile. Place the stitches along a seam at regular intervals. The trick is to work it in groups of 2, 3, or 5 stitches, arranged as half-daisy motifs.

1. Bring the thread up from the back of the fabric. Insert the needle into where it emerged, and bring the point of the needle out a short space away. With the thread wrapped under the needle, pull the needle through the fabric.

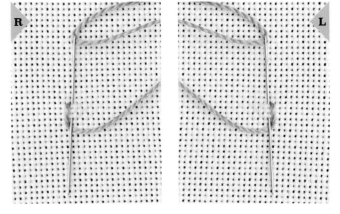

2. Fasten the loop with a small stitch at the bottom.

DETACHED CHAIN-STITCH FLOWER

:: Groups of five detached chain stitches worked along a curved seam

:: Change the direction of the stitch and add some beads, and it becomes more than a simple lazy daisy.

:: You can also work these daisies using silk ribbon. This sample is worked using 2 mm ribbon and a seed bead for the middle.

1. Work a petal at 3 o'clock, 6 o'clock, 9 o'clock, and 12 o'clock.

2. Work a petal between each of the 4 petal stitches from Step 1.

3. Add seed beads or French knots to the middle, and you have a little daisy!

Twisted chain buds are quick and easy and can be effectively introduced in many areas of your block. In this example, a twisted chain stitch is worked using 4 mm silk ribbon to form pink buds tucked between the prongs of the up and down feather stitch.

Twisted chain stitches can be worked in single units or in a line. Twisted chain follows a curve well, so it is very useful for floral motifs and vines; it produces a thorny line that can flow and twist along a seam.

1. Bring the thread up from the back of the fabric and take a stitch so the point emerges a short distance away. Cross the thread over and wrap the thread under the needle.

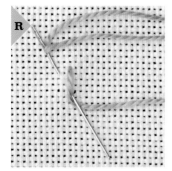 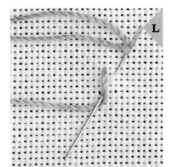

2. Pull the thread through the fabric. As you pull the thread through, notice how you have a loop that is crossed. If you want a single stitch, stop and secure it with a little straight stitch.

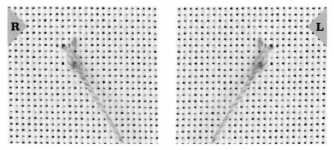

3. If you want to make a line of stitches, insert the needle on the side of the stitch you just made and repeat Steps 1 and 2.

tip If you want to add a little barb to the line, insert the needle close to the previous stitch. If you want a larger barb, insert the needle further away. If you want a particularly thorny-looking line, make the arms of the stitch longer.

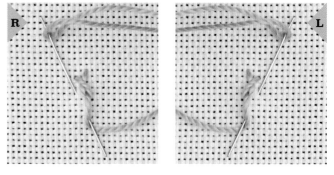

4. Repeat this process along the line.

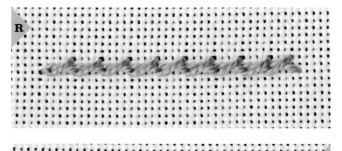

The tremendously versatile detached chain stitch can be worked in dozens of ways. This variation is called a *triple chain*. Use it to easily make little butterflies and winged insects. This simple butterfly can be used as a single motif or as part of a seam embellishment. It is quick and easy, so why not add a whole kaleidoscope of butterflies?

1. Bring the thread up from the back of the fabric. Insert the needle into where it emerged and bring the point of the needle out a short space away. Pull the thread through with the thread wrapped under the needle.

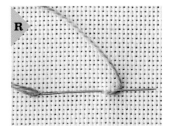

2. For the second stitch, insert the needle into the start of the first chain and take a stitch that is at an angle to the first stitch and is a little longer. With the thread wrapped under the needle, pull the needle through the fabric.

3. Repeat Step 2 to make a third stitch that is a little longer than the second stitch.

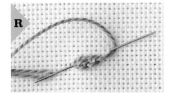
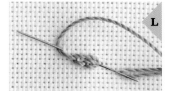

4. You now have half a wing.

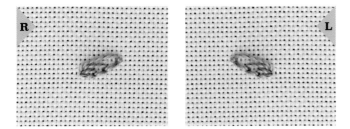

5. Make a second half-wing, being sure that each stitch is even with the stitches on the first half-wing.

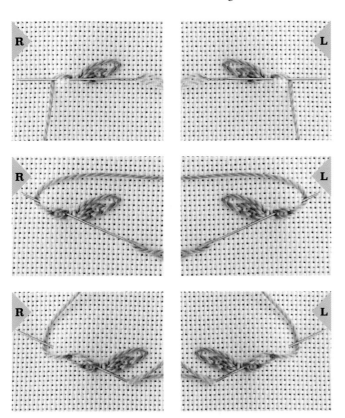

6. You now have 2 wings for an insect.

7. Add a bullion knot for the body, and you have a small motif for a little extra touch in the right place.

> **NOTE**
>
> Once you master the triple chain stitch, you can change the angle of the wings or work a set of four wings with various changes, such as a set of smaller top wings or wings with more extreme angles. Instead of a bullion knot for a body, you can use a bugle bead or three or four seed beads. You can also work this stitch in 2 mm or 4 mm silk ribbon.

Fargo Rose

Fargo rose stitches worked in a large spray. To achieve the color changes in the roses, I used a variegated 7 mm hand-dyed silk ribbon. The leaf stitch leaves were also worked using a variegated hand-dyed ribbon.

Use fargo roses to decorate seams, such as at the peaks of a scallop that was stitched using the stem stitch.

Fargo roses are very effective worked with hand-dyed variegated silk ribbon because they create different-colored roses along a seam.

The fargo rose (or *knot rose*) easily becomes a standard "fall back" stitch to use when designing small sprays or decorating seams.

1. Using 7 mm silk ribbon, bring the thread up from the back of the fabric and wrap it once around the needle about 2″ (5 cm) from where it emerged.

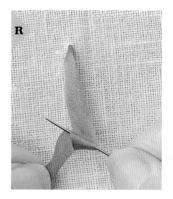 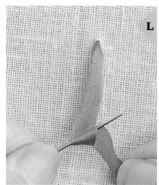

2. Push the tip of the needle through the ribbon about ⅓″ (1 cm) away from the wrap on one side of the ribbon.

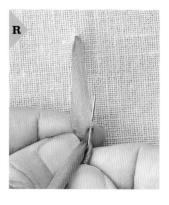 

3. On the opposite side of the ribbon, push the tip of the needle through the ribbon about ⅓″ (1 cm) away, so the needle is zigzagging down the length of the ribbon.

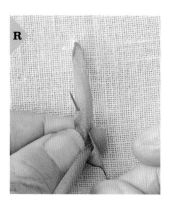 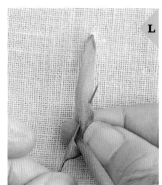

4. This illustrates the path the needle takes. Catch the side of the ribbon. Each step across the ribbon forms a petal. Insert the needle near, but not into, the same place as where the ribbon first emerged from the back.

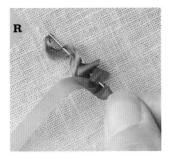 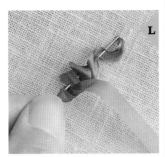

tip For more petals, add more steps. For larger petals, make fewer but longer steps. No matter how many petals you choose, keep the distance between the diagonal steps consistent.

5. Before you take the needle through the fabric, pull the first wrap firmly and slide it down the needle so it is neat. Don't pull too tightly. Just firm it up a little by tugging the tail to create a nice center.

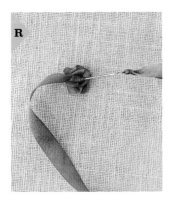 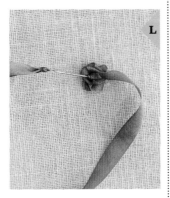

6. With as smooth a motion as possible, pull the needle to the back of the work. This means pulling the needle loaded with the ribbon down the zigzag path, so take it steady. It takes a little practice, but once you get the hang of it they are simple and quick to do.

Fly Stitch

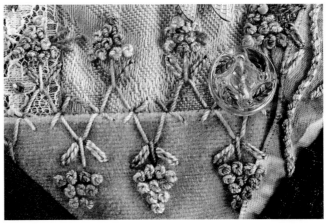

:: Fly stitch worked along a seam as the base of a small floral motif

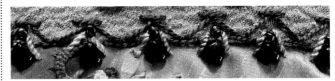

:: Fly stitch used with novelty beads

The fly stitch is very handy because you can easily work a flower bud in the fork of the V. Use 2 bullion knots, a detached chain stitch, a twisted chain stitch worked in silk ribbon, 3 to 5 French knots, a novelty bead, or seed beads to make the bud. The fly stitch is also great in floral sprays or in a line to represent greenery. Little motifs made with the fly stitch can further embellish a line of foundation stitches on a seam. Use hand embroidery thread or 2 mm to 4 mm silk ribbon.

The simple structure of the fly stitch means it can be repeated with ease. You can quickly create a long line of fly stitches and then further decorate them.

1. Bring the thread up from the back of the fabric. Insert the needle to the side and even with where the thread emerged. Take a stitch at a downward angle, so the needle emerges below and between the 2 points.

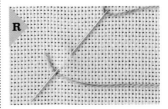 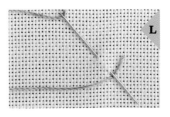

2. With the thread or ribbon wrapped under the needle, pull it through the fabric. Secure the V with a small vertical straight stitch.

French Knot

:: Bunches of blossoms worked in French knots

French knots are tremendously useful to a crazy quilter because they can be used in so many different ways. The thickness of the thread and the number of wraps on the needle determine the size of the finished knot. French knots can also be worked in 2 mm and 4 mm silk ribbon.

tip Stretch your fabric in a needlework hoop or frame so that you have both hands free to work the knot. Use a milliners or straw needle.

1. Bring the thread up from the back of the fabric and place the thread over the needle.

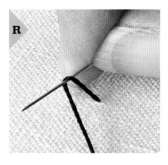

2. Holding the thread taut with your left hand, wrap the thread around the needle 2 or 3 times.

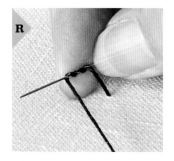
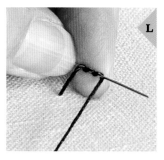

3. Still holding the thread firmly, push the needle back into the fabric, 1 or 2 threads away from where it emerged. Push the knot down the shaft of the needle so it is sitting firmly on the fabric.

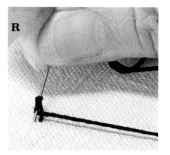
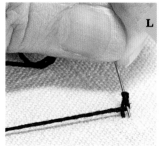

4. Pull the thread through to the back of the fabric. As you pull, use your index finger to hold the thread against the fabric. This helps prevent tangles.

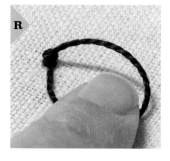

tip If the knot pops to the back of the fabric, take a look at Step 3 again and make sure there is a little fabric between where the needle first emerges and where it reenters. The two points need to be a little ways apart so the knot has some fabric to sit on.

Leaf Stitch

:: Leaf stitches tucked into the fork of feather stitches and worked
:: alongside fargo roses and detached chain stitches

:: Use this stitch for flowers, buds, and leaves. Here, little bud-like
:: motifs appear at the end of a curve of stem stitches.

This stitch is also known as the *Japanese ribbon stitch*.
Quick and easy to work, the ribbon folds in on itself during
the process of stitching, creating the leaf.

1. Bring the ribbon up from the back of the fabric and lay the
ribbon against the fabric (untwisted and flat). Holding the
ribbon flat but not too tight, place the tip of the needle into
the center of the ribbon. This will be the tip of the stitch.

2. Gently pull the needle through the ribbon and the fabric.
Pull until the ribbon folds back on itself and forms a leaf
shape. Don't pull too tight! If you do, the fold will tighten and
go straight through the fabric. Keep your stitches loose for a
natural look.

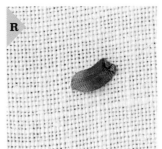 

3. Repeat the process as needed.

Silk ribbon daisies mixed with woven ribbon roses and novelty beads

Silk ribbon daisies with French knot centers on a seam

5-, 6-, and 8-petal flowers are quick and easy using the leaf stitch. I used 7 mm ribbon to demonstrate an 8-petal flower.

1. Mark the fabric for the middle of the flower and the petal points.

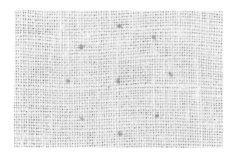

2. Bring the ribbon to the front of the fabric and work the first leaf stitch (See Leaf Stitch, Steps 1 and 2, page 133).

3. Work leaf stitches at 3 o'clock, 6 o'clock, and 9 o'clock.

4. Work a leaf stitch between the stitches created in Step 3.

5. Add a bead in the center and you have a flower!

Straight Stitch

The straight stitch is not complicated. It is as the name suggests—a single stitch.

The straight stitch is a tremendously versatile crazy quilting stitch.

Make straight stitches as needed.

Woven Rose

Woven roses combine well with fargo roses and leaf stitch flowers. This sample is a spray of flowers that tumbles across the bottom of the block.

For this demonstration I used 7 mm silk ribbon.

1. Start with a fly stitch (page 131).

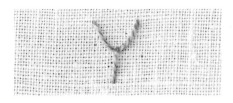

2. Make it into a 5-spoke wheel by adding 2 straight stitches.

3. Bring your needle up at the middle and take it over the first spoke and under the second to start weaving the ribbon through the spokes.

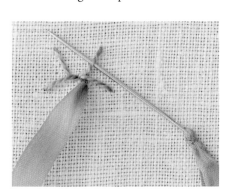

4. Weave your thread over and under the spokes, working outwards.

5. As you weave, do not pull too tight! Let the ribbon fold naturally to form the rose shape. The loose folds produce natural-looking petals. Take care not to pick up any fabric as you do this.

6. When the rose is full, take the needle to the back and finish off. In regular sewing thread, stitch down the ribbon end.

In this sample I mixed woven ribbon roses, fargo roses, and novelty beads. Don't be fearful of letting these types of sprays tumble over the crazy quilt patches.

Another sample where woven roses form part of a floral spray on crazy quilting

part six
Adding Beads, Sequins, Buttons, and Charms to Your Block

After embroidering the seams, motifs, lace, and braids on a crazy block or project, the next step is to add what I call the "hard" embellishments. By hard, I don't mean they are difficult to do—just that as elements, they (things like charms, buttons, and beads) are physically hard. Add these items at the end of the stitching process. If added too soon, the embroidery thread will constantly catch on them and cause tangles. So, to avoid frustration, add them last.

Using Beads, Sequins, and All Those Fun, Shiny Bits!

There is more bling in contemporary crazy quilting than the Victorians used. I think if the Victorians had access to as much material as we do, they would have used it with glee, since the dominant aesthetic of the Victorian period was more, not less. I have never hesitated to use any of the modern products on the market on my crazy quilting, because I see it as a continuation of the tradition.

If you feel a seam is a bit ordinary, add some beads!

However, when adding a mix of beads, buttons, and sequins, think about how they will affect the design. These items introduce more texture and color, and attract the eye. They naturally become a point of emphasis. In most situations, that is what you want, but at other times a hurriedly placed button or a large bead can spoil a good design. It can act in exactly the opposite way you want it to. When this happens, you sense it feels like "too much" or "clashes" with other elements. Moving the button or charm to another position on the block can often solve the problem. If you can't find a home for it, perhaps it is better to leave it off.

This block has a beaded heart-shaped lace motif as the main point of emphasis.

Bugle beads emphasize the zigzag motion of the stitches, which adds more energy to a short seam.

Small beads can be stitched in a line. All lines will act to guide the eye along a path. Beads, because they glitter, have more visual energy and can be used to your advantage.

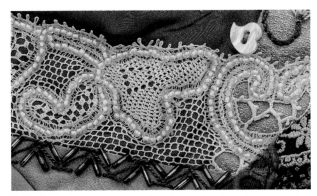

∷ Outline the main pattern of the lace in beads to draw attention
∷ to it.

∷ Beads worked in short lines form the curled stems on this
∷ floral spray.

∷ One way to create a different type of line along a seam is to
∷ sprinkle it with beads, such as the bead trail along the ruffled
∷ ribbon on this block. It creates enough interest in that area to
∷ counter the butterfly and buttons on the other side of the
∷ block.

∷ A small button cluster with a trail of beads leads the eye
∷ elsewhere and takes away the clumped feeling of the buttons.

∷ I balanced a very heavy trail of buttons and beads with bead
∷ tassels falling from two vintage buttons.

When adding buttons and beads, think about scale, color, and shape. In terms of beads, charms, and buttons, these factors influence the composition of a block. They draw the eye from one point in the block to another. One large button in a corner will draw the eye to it. A more dramatic cluster of buttons will do this even more. Use this to your advantage.

tip Try to keep beads well away from the seam allowance and a little inside the block, so that when you piece the blocks together you do not run your sewing machine foot over beads. Use the zipper foot when piecing beaded blocks together.

I used a large vintage button as a point of interest.

A large area of green lace more or less in the middle of a design was causing problems. A dramatic, organic line of buttons clustered in groups solved the problem. Take note of the small lace motif secured by a ring of beads. It draws the eye to that side of the block just enough to make sure that the eye travels around the block and doesn't get stuck on the buttons.

Bead Tassels

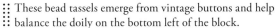
These bead tassels emerge from vintage buttons and help balance the doily on the bottom left of the block.

Smaller bead tassels that have been used along a seam

Bead tassels are fun to make, and people can't resist touching them. They add a real spark to a block.

1. Bring the thread up from the back of the fabric. String 10 to 20 beads onto the needle.

2. Turn the needle, and, skipping the last bead, thread it back up the string of beads.

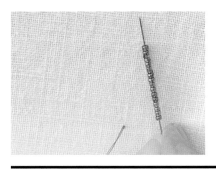

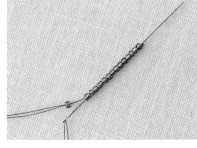

3. Gently pull the thread to tighten the string of beads. Make it snug, but not so tight that it doesn't drape. Insert the needle 1 or 2 threads from where it emerged.

4. Repeat Steps 1–3 to make 3 to 8 strings, depending on the effect you desire. Make a little double-stitch at the back between each string of beads, just in case one ever breaks.

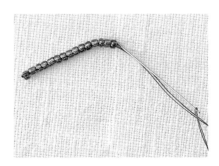

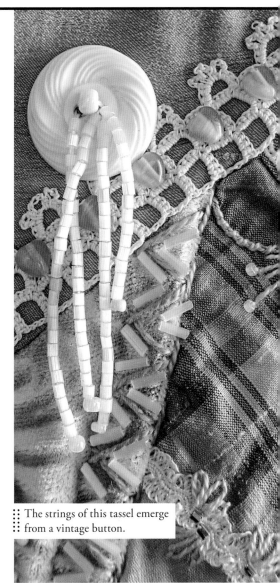
The strings of this tassel emerge from a vintage button.

Using Sequins Creatively

:: Flower-shaped sequins used along a seam and a round sequin
:: secured to the block with bugle beads

:: A similar idea applied to crazy quilting. Here, the same
:: black flower sequin was secured with a novelty bead, and
:: bugle beads were tucked in between the sequin petals.

:: You can extend the basic shape of a sequin by adding beads. A
:: black flower-shaped sequin was secured first with a little round
:: sequin, and then bugle beads were added.

:: Examples of other patterns you can build using the same black
:: flower sequin as the starting point

It is the nature of sequins to be a bit bright and perky.
If you don't want them to dominate, don't set up really
strong contrasts.

Sequins are available in a variety shapes, such as flowers,
stars, hearts, and leaves, and in many sizes. They are fun
to incorporate either along a seam or as a small motif.

tips

• Match the sequin color to a tone in the background.

• Choose small sequins that will not dominate.

• Place other items near the sequins that are more interesting
  and draw the eye away from the sequins.

HOW TO SEW ON SEQUINS

To attach sequins, use a beading needle, a crewel #10 needle, or a straw #10 needle. You can use embroidery thread, polyester/cotton sewing thread, or any decorative thread that will go through the hole of the needle and through the hole in the sequin.

Sequins with a single central hole can be attached by placing a seed bead in the middle. To do this, bring the needle up from underneath the fabric through the hole in the sequin, thread a seed bead onto the thread, and then insert the needle back through the sequin and fabric.

To attach star-, sunburst-, and flower-shaped sequins, use straight stitches that radiate from the center hole.

Sequins of different shapes can be stacked to create a variety of different patterns and motifs. The trick is to contrast the shape or scale of the sequins.

⋮⋮ Small flower-shaped sequins made by stacking different-shaped sequins on top of each other and securing them with a seed bead

Modern sequins are plastic and can be folded or cut. I use a pair of paper scissors, but *not* my embroidery scissors.

⋮⋮ If you look closely at many novelty
⋮⋮ sequins, you will see ways of cutting
⋮⋮ them in order to create something
⋮⋮ different. Here I have cut petals off a
⋮⋮ flower to create a different shape.

⋮⋮ These flower-shaped sequins have been cut. On the first sample, I removed
⋮⋮ one petal of the flower to make a butterfly shape. The other sample is made up
⋮⋮ of flower sequins cut in half and stitched in an alternating line.

⋮⋮ There are many novelty sequins on the market. These sequins
⋮⋮ are domed and quite attractive in their own right.

⋮⋮ Novelty sequins in the shape of flowers secure rickrack along
⋮⋮ a seam.

 tip Most modern sequins are plastic. If you touch them with an iron, they will melt!

Don't Forget to Add a Spider!

∷ The web is made of metallic thread, and the spider is a brass charm.

Traditionally, spiders were included on crazy quilts as a symbol of good luck. I must admit that most of the time I cheat and use charms.

∷ Here a spider is creeping from behind a fargo rose. Make the web a little uneven for a more natural look.

∷ You can also include other insects. In this case, I used butterfly charms along a seam.

When to Stop!

I am often asked, "When do you stop embellishing?" To be honest, this is a tough question, because every stitcher will stop at a different point. It is hard to describe, but at a particular point in the process, a block reads as a complete composition. Each part of the block performs its role in leading the viewer's eye around the block. At some point you start to feel that if you add more, the block will just look crowded and various parts of it will start fighting for attention. That is when you stop.

About the Author

Sharon Boggon has been "fabric-ating" since she was a little girl. She trained in fine arts in Perth, Western Australia, and developed great skill in contemporary embroidery and crazy quilting. She has taught crazy quilting internationally and online, and was a lecturer in the Textiles Department at the Canberra School of Art—part of the Australian National University. She lives in Canberra, Australia's "bush capital," with her woodworking husband. They have one grown daughter who is a circus performer and costume designer.

Want even more creative content?

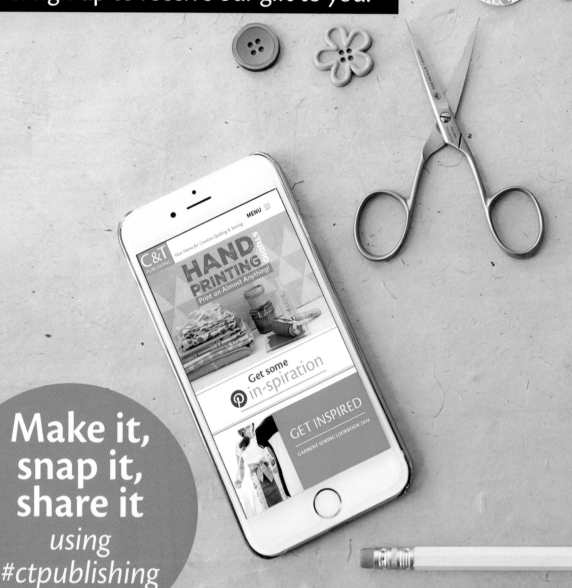

Make it, snap it, share it *using #ctpublishing*